# THE
# CHRISTIAN
# HUSBAND

# THE
# CHRISTIAN
# HUSBAND

## How to Become
## The Husband
## God Wants You to Be

### FRED RENICH

**LIVING LIFE PUBLICATIONS**
Montrose, Pennsylvania

*First Printing — December, 1976*

Copyright © 1976 by Fred C. Renich
All Rights Reserved.
No part of this book may be reproduced without written
permission from the publishers, Living Life Publications,
Montrose, Pennsylvania 18801.


Library of Congress Catalog Card Number: 76-47727
ISBN 0-918018-01-3, cloth.


Scripture quotations, unless otherwise noted, are from the
*American Standard Version* of the Bible and are reprinted with
permission of Thomas Nelson & Sons, © by International
Council of Religious Education, 1929.


*Printed in the United States of America*

*TO* ——
*my wonderful family*
*whose beautiful loyalty*
*and loving honesty have*
*done so much to challenge*
*me to keep growing as a*
*husband and a father.*

# Contents

*Contents*

## Part V — Thoughts on the Why of It All

# Introduction

Each of us is living with at least his second wife! We married an ideal, and we're living with reality!

This book will help you live wholesomely and happily with the *real* girl you married.

There are many books written to help our wives in the impossible task of living with us men. But it's rather strange that relatively few have been written specifically to help us husbands. And, if I'm at all representative, we need help just as much as our wives do.

When Jill wrote her exciting book for wives, *To Have and To Hold*,* she told me I ought to write one for husbands. I said that any book for husbands would have to be different. Men think differently, react differently, and they deal with life's issues differently than women do. But

* Renich, Jill, *To Have and To Hold*, Grand Rapids, Mich., The Zondervan Corporation, 1972

11

*Introduction*

I was sure someone else should or would do the writing. But Jill encouraged me, and gradually ideas began to form. This book is the result.

*The Christian Husband* isn't a marriage manual giving the techniques for a satisfying sex life. That important aspect of marriage has been handled adequately by capable authors. I have tried, rather, to deal with underlying basics. Marriage is so much more than romance. It involves building enduring and endearing relationships between two very imperfect people. But men are usually realists, accustomed to starting with whatever resources are available, and with them creating the fulfillment of their dreams. And that's how God works. He begins where we are and builds from twisted humanity the fabric of an eternal kingdom.

This book is for the Christian husband, because only men who are committed to Jesus Christ and His way of life have access to those divine resources without which it is impossible to make marriage work as God planned it should.

Throughout these pages I have shown that happy, wholesome homes *can* be built out of the raw material of fallen human nature — but *only* as Christ is central in the building process.

Since building takes work and persistence, I have given practical assignments for you to work out in your daily living. It will help if you keep paper and pen handy as you read. Jot down areas you will want to work on, and don't put off doing the exercises. They are designed to help you implement the principles referred to.

Above all, ask God to give you the ability to be honest with yourself and your situation. With families coming

12

unglued all over the place, you can't afford to be casual about your own home and what it is becoming with you as its husband and leader.

This book is the distillation of over thirty years of building our own marriage. We are more sure than ever that lasting marriages don't just happen. But to express in readable form the dynamics involved in that building process has not been easy. I owe so much to the encouragement and inspiration of my wife Jill and our loyal, enthusiastic, and refreshingly open and honest young people: Jan and Bobby, Rosalie and Robb, Rick, and youngest daughter Lyn. They've been a part of the project from its beginning, and I am grateful for their encouragement, prodding, and constructive criticism, in addition to hours spent in correcting and typing the manuscript. I am indebted to Sue Murray for the final typing and preparation of the manuscript and to Sarah Bertsch for hours of proof reading.

Is anything worthwhile ever accomplished without many hands being involved? That's what the kingdom of God is all about — Christ and His own living and working together — each for the good and blessing of the other. That's how happy families are built, too! Each of us living, not for ourselves, but for each other.

One final suggestion: After you've read this book yourself, why not use it as the basis for a series of discussions in a men's group or with a group of couples? The material on these pages will stimulate interesting and fruitful discussion.

Fred Renich
Montrose, Pennsylvania
December, 1976

# Part I

Basics

# 1

## Let's Face It — God Is There!

Whether we like it or not, God *is* at the center of things! We don't have to admit it, or even believe it. What we do with it doesn't change the fact that, "In the beginning (and all the way through life and history) — God. . ."

The world, and things in it like trees and fields, mountains and oceans, birds, animals, and man . . . these were all God's idea. You didn't make yourself, nor did I. Not one of us asked to be put here, and not one of us can guarantee how long we'll stay. Some people stay around quite awhile, others check out before they've hardly started. A lot of times it doesn't seem to make sense. But it does make sense to recognize and accept the obvious and the unalterable — God and His primacy in the facts of life, especially as they relate to you and me and our brief stint on the world's stage.

But I thought this was a book for husbands!

You're right. But you can't talk about the husband part until you've talked about the man, and it's rather naive to talk about either the man or the husband unless you do it on the backdrop of the One Who is at the center of it all — God. Even such common things as women, marriage, children and home — these were all God's idea. If I could put it very simply, God was the first "marry'n parson." He performed the first wedding. He established the first home. Life is complicated enough as it is. Let's not make it more so by trying to sort out life while ignoring the key to it all — that Wonderful, Mighty, Eternal, Righteous and Loving Person — God.

The family, as God planned it, was designed to function harmoniously. That first home was a bit of heaven on earth. Living for each other was as natural as breathing, because that ugly thing called selfishness was still foreign to the new-born race.

Our ideals for family and home are rooted in those early God-created beginnings. Just as each individual has an inner feeling that he ought to be a better person, so most of us feel marriage ought to work a lot more easily and effectively than it does.

Why is love so fragile?

We know a lot of marriage hassles are really our own fault. Then why do we have them?

Some people are suggesting we ought to forget the whole marriage idea and just live together! But that doesn't really work either, because inevitably someone gets hurt in the process.

The difficulties, problems and impossibles of marriage weren't God's plan. Something terrible happened. Man himself messed up the plan by his own free, deliberate choice. But God knows it happened — and it hasn't *thrown Him or His plan.* If we're going to find answers to life as it is today, we need to know a little about the root problem which started a long, long time ago!

# 2

# A Look at the Control Package

## Man Isn't Programmed

Pigs are interesting creatures, in spite of all the mean thoughts people have about them. At least they won't dig their graves with their teeth, and that's more than we can say about some people! What's more, a pig will balance his own diet if you feed him his dietary components in different dishes.

Where did the oriole go to school to learn how to weave such a delightful little nest that hangs so delicately from the forked twig way up in the tree? But it couldn't build a robin's nest if its life depended on it! Birds fly south in the fall, and nobody taught them how to find their way. They don't fly east or west, and they couldn't learn if they tried.

It's obvious the animal world operates on the basis of built-in instinctive controls. But not man. Endowed as he is with the fantastic dynamics of mind, will, emotion, appetite, and life drives, he is without a built-in control package. This is one of the fundamental differences between man and the animals. God designed man as a person, who in the intimacy of a voluntary love-relationship with God as his Lord, would experience God as his "control system." Of course there are similarities between man and animals. Both are physical beings, designed to function in a physical world. But man is far more than just a physical being. While housed in a physical body which has physical functions, man as a person is so far above the animals that it is blasphemous to suggest there is any true relationship between them.

Man as a person was created in the image of God. He was intended by God to be the vehicle for expressing in tangible ways through his personality and his body the beauty and wonder of the character of the invisible God. As an old saint of a past generation put it:

> "Man was created for higher purposes than to make his body a strainer for meat and drink and to fatten up a banquet for worms."

To live to eat might do for oxen, but it won't do for man. His reason for being is so much deeper, his destiny is so much higher, and as one would expect, his abilities and capacity are infinitely greater.

When God placed our first parents on the earth, He gave them a job to do. In simple terms that first job description stated:

> "Be fruitful, and multiply, and replenish the earth, and subdue it; and have dominion over the fish of the sea, and over the birds of the heavens, and over every living thing that moveth upon the earth."                    Genesis 1:28

21

Man was to rule this world for God. He was to be God's regent in a physical world; to look after God's interests in the world God had made.

Man's reason for being must be worthy of his nature and his abilities. Created in the image of God, he was to demonstrate in his person and activities the character of God. Endowed by God with capacity and abilities in harmony with man's lofty nature, he was to be lord of the world in which God placed him — to rule as a king under the One Who was Himself both the Origin and on-going Source of man's life and immortal being.

# 3

# Now That the System's Twisted...

### Depravity Is Real

Like a thunderclap the blow fell, and man found himself, not lord of his world but its slave. With those awful words of God's judgment ringing in their ears, our first parents found themselves locked out of the Paradise in which they had been placed. A flaming sword barred any hope of a return to their former condition, work, or intimate fellowship with the God whose smile and companionship they had so recently enjoyed.

"Unto Adam He said: Because thou hast harkened unto the voice of thy wife, and hast eaten of the tree of which I commanded thee, saying, thou shalt not eat of it: cursed is the ground for thy sake; in toil shalt thou eat of it all the days of thy life; thorns also and thistles shall it bring forth to thee; and thou shalt eat the herb of the field; in the sweat of thy face shalt thou eat bread, till thou return unto the

ground; for out of it wast thou taken; for dust thou art, and
unto dust shalt thou return.

"So he (God) drove out the man; and he placed at the east
of the garden of Eden the Cherubim, and the flame of a
sword which turned every way, to keep the way of the tree
of life."                                          Genesis 3:17–19, 24

In keeping with the lofty nature with which man was
endowed at creation was the awesome power of personal
freedom to choose. Our first parents were not locked into
a predetermined way of life by some control-mechanism
forced upon them by their Creator. That will do for nature and the animals who are a part of it. They live their
lives and fulfill their purpose for being, not by choice, but
by built-in laws which govern their existence. But man
was created in God's image. And a part of God's nature is
His own free will. He is not a self-contained pre-set mech-
anism that *must* operate according to an unalterable predetermined pattern. God is holy and He is always that
way. But He is holy because He loves what is right, always!

We say God can't do wrong, but in the sense in which
people usually mean it, the statement is not true. We
should say God *won't* do wrong. He does what is right,
*always,* because He loves what is right. This power of free
choice lies at the very heart of the nature of God. For
man to be created in God's image involves this same freedom. But where there is no opportunity to choose an al-
ternative *there is no freedom.*

For man to fulfill his reason for being he must
choose as his way of life that which is central to his nature — the image of God. He must choose it both because

24

it is right and because he loves it. Central to that image of God, (with which man is endowed) is the acceptance of the unalterable reality that God is the *only* Self-existent Being. All others, including man, are dependent beings.

This was the heart of that horrible tragedy in the Garden of Eden. Man, in his deliberate choice to disobey God really chose to be independent of God. In other words, he chose to be his own god. Instantly, a strange new awareness possessed him. He didn't want God around, but ran from Him and hid. Adam and Eve also felt compelled to hide from each other by covering themselves. In that brief moment they discovered that Eden was much more than a perfect place. It was at root a right relationship to the One who created and sustained Eden, themselves and the whole created world. As soon as their relationship to God was broken, *what had been a heaven began to be hell.*

At the heart of man's being there is now a fatal distortion. Selfishness, a twisted self-love, is the foul disease that has doomed man to slavery, mortality, death and decay. Having chosen as he did, there is now no way for man to live. Death is inevitable, for man is voluntarily at war with the Source of life. He has chosen as his god a created, temporal and dependent world, and has rejected the Creator, God, who alone is eternal and eternally self-existent.

In response to man's fatal choice God acted, not in wrath but in love.

"Cursed is the ground *for your sake.* . ."

"In toil shall you eat of it all the days of your life. . ."

". . thorns and thistles shall it produce for you. In the

25

sweat of your face shall you eat bread. . . *until* you return to the ground, for out of it were you taken."

"for dust you are, and unto dust you shall return. . ."

Man became mortal.

His world turned to ashes.

What he chose as the road to glorious self-fulfillment he must discover, in experience, to be the fatal path to blasted hopes, unrealized dreams, misery, despair, and oblivion!

Remember the glittering lie of a promise the tempter held out to our first parents? In reality he told them:

"Don't really believe what God has told you. In that prohibition he gave you (forbidding you to eat the luscious fruit of this tree), He's just keeping you under and making sure HE stays top dog! Why, He *knows*, (but has deliberately lied to you) that eating this fruit will give you true liberty and open the door for you to experience full self-realization. Listen friends, I'll tell you a secret: Go ahead and assert your independence. Forget this God's commands. Strike out on your own. Take it from me, YOU WON'T DIE. Instead, you'll LIVE!!!   And — YOU WILL BE LIKE GOD!"

Man took the bait. He believed the lie. Truth was rejected and falsehood embraced. How tragic and fatal the consequences were!

However, the tragedy was so much deeper than what appeared on the surface. It consisted in a fundamental distortion in man's philosophy of life. Created a dependent being, he imagined himself an independent, self-existent being. He turned from dependence on God as his very life and expected to find life in himself and in the created world around him. He turned to "worship and

26

serve the creature rather than the Creator. . ." Romans 1:25

I don't understand *why* God chose to redeem His rebellious, self-estranged creation, but He did. He could have wiped the slate clean right at the start to begin all over again. But He chose a different route and a far more difficult one.

God chose to win man back to Himself by loving man in his rebellion and sin. *The first expression of that love* was to place His (God's) whole beautiful world under the pall of a curse, to make the temporal world less appealing to man's wayward heart. Until man's redemption is completed, God refused to allow nature to be what it can be — beautiful and bountiful beyond comprehension. At the same time He commuted the awful sentence of eternal death which automatically fell upon man. Instead of declaring the sentence of doom, God chose to bear in His own person the awful stroke of execution — to die for man, the just for the unjust, to bear in His own body the punishment for man's sin — yours and mine!

What really *is* redemption? In addition to forgiveness for all of our sins, it is nothing less than God's mighty love winning the *voluntary, ever deepening trust and affection of our hearts*. Without this even His pardon would be inadequate, for until we come to *trust* God and *love* HIM there can be no heaven for us. Heaven would be hell without love. The chief glory of heaven is that same wonderful God whom Satan represented to our first parents as evil. Only those who love God for who He is — holy in His character, perfect in His ways, and Lord of all things created and uncreated — only those people could be happy in heaven.

27

The big question is: Where is your heart? What does it love? Toward what does it gravitate?

Ultimately, you will do what you love to do. Each of us follows his own heart to the degree that we are not hindered by outside factors. Sooner or later God will permit circumstances to arrange themselves so that our actions *will demonstrate* where our heart really is.

This is why the curse is such a blessing. God loves us too much to let us have perfection in this world. It's tough enough to keep from being attached to the world and life in its fallen state. What would it be like if we were in a perfect environment?

That's right. The system's twisted. Not just a part of it, but all of that which is a part of this earthly and human scene. And the twist is not only out there in nature, where beetles and bugs, drought and famine, disease, suffering and death appear to hold undisputed sway. It is right at the very heart of your nature and mine. The twist is real. There is a ruling principle that dominates every one of us — *selfishness.*

That's just a synonym for what the Bible calls sin.

If we are going to find answers for our own lives as well as for our varied relationships in life, we'll have to start by accepting the difficult, tough, unpleasant but real fact — selfishness is there — in me, in you, and in everyone around us, including our wives and our children.

We must also recognize that every other person will have the same essential battles to face, and answers to find, as we have. They too must discover for themselves that *only* God can bring their hearts to love Him more than themselves, and to love His ways more than their self-centered ways. Unless God works a change, their hearts (as well as ours) will remain attached to a cursed and perishing world — loving and serving the creature rather than the Creator. As we automatically expect them to be patient with us, so we also must accept our responsibility to be patient and understanding with them.

*We are called to see marriage work beneficially and happily even though the system is twisted.*

That's what the rest of this book is about.

# 4

# The Secret of Measuring Up

**Not More Trying, but Simpler Trusting**

"Look, I've tried so many times to be what I should be, but always with the same result — a miserable failure! Judy thinks I don't care. What she doesn't know is how miserable I am over my sense of constant defeat. My "don't care" attitude is just a cover-up for my guilt feelings of failure.

"When I accepted Christ as my Saviour, they told me He would make me a good Christian if I would follow Him faithfully. But the more I try, the worse things seem to get. I know it's wrong to blow my stack at my wife and kids. But for some reason, when she nags me with her critical voice, it's like something snaps inside. I lose control, and — bang!

"Really, I *have* tried. But I guess this being a Christian just isn't for me. It's probably O.K. for strong people, and for guys who have patient, understanding wives, but for me, well, somehow I just don't seem to be able to measure up.

My Christian friends tell me I don't try hard enough. They're probably right. But I'm not sure they understand what I have to put up with, either."

The trouble is that Jim *and* his friends have missed the way. The secret of measuring up is not to "try harder" but to "lean heavier."

The heart of man's sin is independence.

The heart of man's salvation is dependence.

That's why Christ said:

"Whosoever shall not receive the kingdom of God as a little child, he shall in no wise enter therein."     Luke 18:17

Our biggest battle is to learn how to *be like little children* — dependent. We get flashes of this in our Christian experience, but *dependence must become a way of life,* as automatic as the attitude of expectant trust in the life of a child. Most of us came to the place of helplessness and dependence in the process and act of receiving Christ as our Saviour. But this dependence was related primarily to the horrible reality of past sin, guilt, a holy God, and our need for forgiveness and acceptance by Him. We were taught clearly that we had to come to Christ just as we were. We had to come trusting Him completely to accept us as sinners for whom He had died, and whom He was willing to forgive fully. All of this we were to do on the condition that we stop *trying* to save ourselves and turn instead to rely on Him alone for our eternal salvation.

But those same instructors who taught us how to come to Christ in simple dependence (faith) failed to tell us that life was to be lived each day on the *same* basis! We were taught rather to "wrestle against our corrupt na-

31

ture," to "follow Christ faithfully," and "work hard at being Christians." In other words, having been saved by grace through faith, we were now to grow by performing acceptable works.

For many of us, including Jim, this was followed by a weary round of dedications, resolutions, determinations — some slight success, and then — failure. Christian magazines, books, sermons and glowing testimonies from "successful" Christians kept coming through with the idea that if a person really "had what it takes" he too would be able to join the band of victorious, productive, "with it" Christians.

Does this mean we just lie down in despair and quit? No! The way you became a Christian was to come to Christ just as you were, lost and undone, with no ability to save yourself, but WITH THE CONFIDENCE THAT CHRIST WOULD SAVE YOU *IN THE ACT OF YOUR COMING.*

We are not to look at our helplessness, but at His adequacy. The fact is we never *really* turn to His adequacy *until* we have looked at our helplessness. But we musn't stop with looking at ourselves. It is trust in Christ that saves initially, and *it is trust in Christ that brings the victory in each succeeding step along the way.*

When we talk about trusting Him, we are not thinking of mere "hoping." True faith *"expects Christ to do what we are counting on Him to do."* Many of us wistfully "hope" He will undertake for us, and when He doesn't we tend to say or think: "There, I thought it wouldn't work." Then we lapse back again into trying somehow to be good Christians.

When you came to Christ initially, you knew that if

He failed you would be finished as far as any hope of getting to heaven was concerned. In the same way you have to recognize that if Christ doesn't "come good" in terms of your day-by-day Christian life, you will be a failure. And when you *do* fail, you need to go right back to Christ and tell Him that in this instance HE DID NOT COME GOOD! Tell Him, since He *is* true, His promises *are* true, and His purpose to make you a man well-pleasing to God remains firm, *then you are still counting on Him to "come good" in your life.*

In Hebrews 10:35, 36 we are told:

"Cast not away therefore your boldness, which hath great recompense of reward. For ye have need of patience (steadfastness), that, having done the will of God, ye may receive the promise." (i.e. the fulfillment of the thing promised)

The "will of God" in this passage is the exercise of counting on God, believing that He will come good in a given matter, or expecting Him to do what He has promised. And the command is for us to hold steady with patience and expectation UNTIL GOD RESPONDS.

What Jim was really saying is that he couldn't be what he should be until his wife changed. But God wanted Jim to learn that Christ is adequate to demonstrate His victory in Jim's life regardless of whether his wife changed or not.

If you are "Jim" take a few minutes to ask yourself what it is specifically in your wife that gets to you. There may be many things about her that bother you, but there's probably one thing that's the key problem.

Remember, God knows about that problem just as

well as you do. If it's something bad, He's not pleased with it any more than you are. The difference is you get uptight about it, and God doesn't. Her negative turns your love into resentment, gets you upset, impatient, unhappy, and then you probably blow up. In contrast, her negatives don't cause God to stop loving her, understanding her, or being patient and gracious to her. Because God remains objective in the presence of her negatives, He is able to see clearly the best way to bring about needed changes in her. Since you get upset and emotionally involved because of her negatives you only complicate the total problem.

You want your wife to change.

God wants you both to change.

You are saying: "God, get my wife straightened out and I'll be O.K."

God is saying: "I understand how you feel, but I'm using your wife to show you your need for me to change you. Your wife doesn't *make you* what you are. She only brings out of you what was there all the time. If you will let Me, I will make you so victorious *that your relationship toward your wife, as she is, will be just like my loving relationship is to both of you, as you are.*"

What is the key thing in your wife that sets you off? In honesty of heart take it to God and tell Him you are giving it to Him for Him to take care of in His way and time. Also tell God you are starting right now to count on Him to make you react to that negative in your wife just like He, God, reacts to it — with loving composure. Remind God that if and when He fails to work for you at any time when your wife's negative starts bugging you, then you will respond like you always have. But even so, you still choose to believe God is true, as He has stated:

> ". . . they that wait for (trust in) Me shall not be put to shame."                                    Isaiah 49:23b

Make today an adventure of bold anticipating trust.

Look for a miracle to happen in your attitude.

Remember, light is needed only in darkness. God intends for us to shine in the dark. If He took the darkness away (like your wife's negative), then you couldn't shine!

A lamp doesn't struggle to shine. It only transmits as light what comes from the power source.

You don't struggle to be victorious! You only transmit (by dependence on Christ) that victorious life which comes from Him . . . Your Power Source!

I am not suggesting this will come easily or in one beautiful instantaneous moment. For me it has taken time — years. But steadily and surely it is becoming a way of life.

But this way of life had a beginning. It began when I really accepted the *fact* that changing me (and our marriage) was God's business. I saw my part was to expect Him to do it issue by issue, circumstance by circumstance, moment by moment and day by day. I recall telling myself years ago:

> "Renich, you just don't have it. If succeeding as a Christian husband depends on you, forget it. But surely, Lord, You are big enough to manage me. And I thank You that You will, whether Jill ever changes or not."

From then on, He has been faithful to motivate me to face specific issues in my personal life and in our marriage that forced me to trust Him rather than struggle in my own miserable weakness.

My own experience is described so beautifully in Proverbs 4:18:

> "The path of the righteous is as the dawning light, that shineth more and more unto the perfect day."

Don't be afraid of *starting* to walk the path of trust. Remember you only need to take —

*One Step at a Time!*

# 5

# The First Person You Meet Is You

## To Live with Others You Must
## First Live with Yourself

How much are you worth? A hundred dollars? One thousand? Ten thousand or a million?

Maybe you have never put a dollar sign beside your name, but has God?

The Bible teaches that we have been purchased — redeemed. That means God paid something for us. Value was given for the item purchased.

How much did God pay for you?

How about stating a dollar figure?

"Impossible," you say.

Yes! Because the price God paid for you and for me is beyond computation.

". . . ye were redeemed, not with corruptible things, with silver or gold, . . . but with precious blood, as of a lamb without blemish and without spot, even the blood of Christ."                                    I Peter 1:18, 19

You don't pay that kind of money for junk —
unless — the junk has potential!

So now, how much are you worth? Plenty! Fantas-
tically plenty!

Then why do you keep telling yourself you're worth-
less?

Since God has decided you're valuable, you had better agree — and start looking at yourself that way!

"Yes, but what about all the rotten negatives I see in
myself?"

Don't you think God knows about them? Did He
purchase you with His eyes shut? Or did He not know exactly what He was getting when He purchased you?

Yes, He did, and in spite of all the negatives, He still
paid heaven's fortune for you.

You *are* valuable!

The facts are, man — a seeming pile of twisted
junk — has potential. He is redeemable. God sees that
man can be remade into something beautiful, like God's
character. Instead of rejecting man as hopeless, fit only
for the trash heap, God sees every negative in man as an
opportunity for His redemptive transforming power.

That's why God accepts us.

He loves us for what we can be.

He intends to make us exhibitors of His recreative
love and power.

The starting point with God is that He accepts us as
we are, in order to make us what He knows we can be.

Our starting point with ourselves is for us to accept
ourselves as we are, with the recognition that God is
going to make us what He sees we can become.

In the run-of-the-mill of daily life, the first person

38

you always meet is — you! At every turn of the road you are there. When you get up in the morning or the last thing at night, it is you that you have to live with. And *what you are to others is determined by what you are to yourself.*

Misery loves company. And no miserable man can stand happy people around him. The only way for him to be happy is to make those around him miserable. Since his closest associates are his family they are the first ones to suffer.

Next to having a genuine relationship to God, you and I must have a right relationship to ourselves. Both of these relationships, to God and to ourselves, form the foundation upon which the relationship to our families is built. Show me a man who is at peace with God *and* himself, and he is almost sure to be wholesome and positive toward his family.

An adequate husband is *the* expression of a genuine Christian and a maturing person.

Since God has accepted us as we are, why do we have such difficulty accepting and living with ourselves? Two reasons stand out as fairly obvious.

First, we confuse acceptance with approval. It's a basic law that all progress must begin from where one is at a given point. This is true in every area of life. Teachers recognize this. Tradesmen, mechanics, doctors — yes, even God recognized this basic truth. But acceptance of a situation doesn't mean approval of it. God accepts us as sinners, but He doesn't approve of our sin. The teacher accepts the pupil, but he doesn't approve of the pupil's ignorance. The doctor accepts the patient, but he doesn't approve of the disease.

Actually, genuine acceptance has purpose to it. The

39

teacher accepts the pupil in order to teach him what he aspires to learn, and the doctor accepts his patient in order to effect a cure. God accepts us to make us better people.

If we could grasp this point clearly, it would help us to be more free toward ourselves. We cannot approve of our sinfulness, but we can accept it in order to see it change.

The second reason it's hard for us to accept ourselves is that we identify our negative expressions with ourselves as persons. We know certain attitudes and behavior patterns are wrong. But instead of rejecting the wrong attitude or wrong acts of behavior, we reject ourselves.

A husband shared with me his feelings of guilt because he enjoyed looking at a woman's figure. But this problem was compounded by his hatred of himself (self-rejection) for being, as he put it, a "dirty minded person."

\* \* \* \* \*

An attractive college girl told me, "If people knew who I really am, they wouldn't want to be around me." Then she told the very common story of a perfectly normal young lady who had slipped on an icy stretch of life's road and wound up in a moral entanglement. But identifying her indescretion with herself as a person, she not only rejected her actions as evil, but herself as evil also. Consequently, all she could do was hide, cover up, run from herself and from others and all the while hope that no one would discover what an evil person she was.

\* \* \* \* \*

A young man was deeply in love with his sweetheart. Emotion carried them both beyond the bounds of propriety on one of their dates. Identifying his imprudent actions with himself he so condemned, rejected, and hated himself that he nearly ruined the prospects of their relationship.

How can we learn to live with ourselves when we know we are far from perfect? Can I really hate my sin but accept myself, the sinner? If so, how?

*The first step is to clarify the picture.* Most of us live in generalities and vagueness. These often are the root of confusion, discouragement and despair. In the diagram below, the arrows originating from the center of the circle represent reactions to life situations. These situations come to us one at a time, and are seen as arrows on the outside directed to the circle.

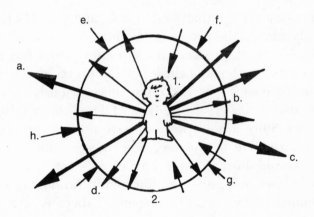

1. The real me inside of the external me.
2. The external me.
   a., b., c., d. — Reactions to life situations.
   e., f., g., h. — Life situations confronting me one at a time and eliciting responses.

The sincere Christian finds it very painful to face his sinful and negative reactions to life as it comes to him via circumstances. He tends to suppress, ignore or try to forget those reactions. The more vivid ones can't be suppressed or forgotten so they remain clearly etched on his memory: the deep disappointment, the bitter sorrow, or the experience of wonderful joy. But there are thousands of reactions that occur every day which barely break the circumference of consciousness. Many of these are known only to the individual himself, remaining unrecognized even by his closest associates. In the Sermon on the Mount, Jesus speaks of the nature of unseen sins, like hateful thoughts, lustful looks, coveteousness, and ulterior motives. (Matthew 6, 7)

The knowledge that God is holy and that He hates evil only adds to the problem. My numerous and adverse reactions seem to proclaim my sinfulness and I feel that God rejects me. I may believe the Scriptures that Christ lives in me (Colossians 1:27), but subconsciously I say to myself that it can't really be true while all this sinning is going on. Since a holy God can have no fellowship with sin, how can He live in me, side by side with temper, worry, hatred, lust, gluttony, etc., etc.?

When we find ourselves defeated in various attempts to eliminate these negative responses, there is only one way to maintain some semblance of composure — hide from them and refuse to face them. We can do this by suppression, forgetting, ignoring, or even denying that they exist.

This process is helped immeasurably by shifting our attention from the reactions themselves to the situations that brought them on. But at root, all we are doing is adding self-deceit to the total list of personal sins. Instead of being helped, the problem is compounded. The result is clearly seen in the case of Jim who quieted his own troubled conscience by shifting his attention and blame to his wife, saying in effect:

"If Judy would be different, I'd be O.K."

In a larger sense we are all saying: "If the world would be perfect, I could be a good victorious Christian."

There are times when the dishonesty of escapism is not enough. Periodically we are caught. Then we are forced to admit some obvious sinful act. How do we react? Do we then bring the matter immediately to God, confess it candidly, claim His promised forgiveness, and rise immediately to praise Him for His redeeming love and go on our way rejoicing?

No! We have to grovel for awhile. We feel, look, and act miserable. There is a feeling that it would be sacrilegious to rejoice and praise too soon. Subconsciously we are saying God has left us, gone back to His heaven to stay until we have done a certain amount of personal atoning. Only when this is done, whether it takes three hours or three days, do we dare believe God returns to re-establish His residence in the center of our life.

What we fail completely to see is that:

1. God (in Christ) lives within our mixed up lives for the purpose of dealing with our negative and sinful reactions.
2. His way is to deal with one issue at a time — not with everything at once.

43

3. He can only deal with a sinful or negative reaction:
   - *When it happens*
   - *On Location*
   - *Within the You or Me from which the reaction arises.*

This is why it's imperative that we learn:

1. To be completely honest with ourselves about ourselves.
2. To resist the temptation to focus on our circumstances as the cause of our sinful reactions.
3. To *refuse to yield to self-rejection or despair* when we react wrongly to life situations.

While it may be unpleasant to face up to my reactions in life, there is no other way that will lead me to the goal of true personal freedom.

A couple of simple exercises may help.

On a sheet of paper make two lists side by side, leaving space between the two colums. To the left make a list of your strengths. To the right make a list of your weaknesses. Under each strength and weakness indicate one recent situation which illustrates the validity of your evaluation of that behavior pattern. In addition, draw lines connecting any strength that is related to a corresponding weakness.

| Strengths | Weakness |
| --- | --- |
| | |
| | |
| | |
| | |
| | |

You may finish with something like this:

| | |
|---|---|
| kind | self-indulgent |
| gentle | too easy-going |
| patient | backed off from spanking disobedient child<br>indecisive |
| relaxed | lazy |
| didn't get uptight in rush hour traffic | |

Study your list. Do you see that every strength is a basis for a corresponding weakness? And every weakness is a potential strength?

For example, the kind and gentle father may find it hurts himself too much to spank his child. What is a wonderful strength may actually show up as being weakness when his gentle spirit is confronted by a situation calling for firmness and necessary correction.

Out of your total list, select one strength and one weakness:

1. List several instances when you have let your strength express itself in weakness.
2. List any specific steps you have taken to correct the weakness.
3. List some steps which you believe would help you avoid expressing the strength as weakness.

Now look at the whole list again:

1. Check each strength for which you have thanked God. If you haven't thanked Him, stop now and do so.

45

2. Check each weakness which you actually believe God *is going to rectify.*

   a. List at least one scripture reference that supports your belief that God is going to do this.

   b. Have you thanked God that He will do it. How often do you do this? If you haven't thanked Him, will you do it now?

3. What do you propose doing about those weaknesses which you aren't sure God will correct?

4. Again, take one weakness which you believe God is going to correct:

   a. List one or more ways you think He may or could use to bring about improvement.

   b. Think again of the type of situation which stimulates this weakness. *Would it really help you if God changed the situation before you changed?*

We have been talking about getting a clear, honest, objective picture of ourselves and of God in relation to us as we really are. In this process it's most important that we see and accept the facts as they are:

1. God bought us "as is" with full knowledge of everything about us, both positive and negative.

2. His acceptance of what He bought is purposeful.

3. He has demonstrated His acceptance of us by making our lives His dwelling place. *He does not leave us* each time one of our negatives shows up in a sinful reaction to life-circumstances.

4. Since God lives in us with purpose (to make us what we can be) then we *must* be content to live with ourselves and not "run away" whenever we miss the boat.

The second step in learning to live with our imperfect selves is to start walking by faith (dependence) rather than by struggle.

It is always painful to learn to walk. It never seems to come easily, whether for the infant toddler or for an adult who, because of accident or illness must relearn the art. Theoretically it's very simple. A person walks by placing one foot in front of another in a series of steps. No person ever takes more than one step at a time.

To walk by faith means taking one step at a time. This is another way of saying we choose to be dependent in one situation at a time. Along with choosing to be dependent, we choose to act rightly in a spirit of dependence on God in that situation.

As a Sunday School teacher, I felt it was important to get to Sunday School a few minutes before the opening exercises began.

While to most people I seemed like a rather placid, easy going person, I had a thing about being on time and early when I had responsibilities. The slightest lateness was really frustrating, although I kept this quite well covered, except to my family.

For years, I struggled with my resentments over Jill's tendency to be late. I knew my uptightness was sin — but try as I would to be relaxed, whenever I saw we were arriving late I'd get tense.

One day I began to comprehend the real meaning of that truth, "the just shall live by faith." I saw how the attitude of dependence on God was to operate in *all* of life, not just in the area of being forgiven and saved for heaven. I accepted as a present reality the fact that God had accepted me "as was"; that the Lord Jesus actually lived in me, right alongside all of my weakness, but that He lived there for the purpose of changing old wrong patterns of life into new God-honoring patterns.

As these truths began to grip my mind I became increasingly sensitive to *how* I reacted to the whole of life, even to what I had regarded as insignificant situations.

One Sunday morning the family was caught up in the usual hectic rush to get away in time for Sunday School. I was ready early but the family seemed to be dragging their feet as usual. Sitting in the car and trying with extreme difficulty to be patient, I suddenly saw what it meant to trust *in a specific way.* The understanding came with such clarity that I could almost outline the steps involved.

1. I had to give the whole situation to the Lord, *including* my mounting impatience. This meant I had to leave in God's hands the whole issue of my deep commitment to promptness.
2. I had to accept inward peace from God by faith, and by an act of the will refuse to agree to indulge in impatience.
3. Free from emotional involvement I found myself checking to see whether there was some way in which I could help the others get ready. (There was!)
4. With my spirit free, a new freedom was felt by my family. Wasteful and resented haste and push were replaced by a quiet quickness, and to my amazement we arrived in time and *in a Christian spirit!*

You can see by this illustration I was not passive. In fact, I was more actively involved in getting myself and my family to Sunday School than before I learned to trust. But the activity was totally different and vastly more productive. Before, I sat in the car stewing and getting more and more resentful. Or, if I tried to be helpful, my spirit was so negative and pushy I only made the situation worse. But now, having chosen to be and act in dependence on Christ, I was free and victorious in my spirit. In that freedom I was able to act helpfully and for everyone's good.

Trusting the Lord *in a given situation* sets you free from self-interest and self-concern and provides both the basis and motivation to act appropriately. Regardless of what the circumstance may be, the basic issues are the same. And walking by faith is just repeating over and over again the same things you did when you took one step by faith: like when I discovered how to be at peace in a circumstance which always made me tense.

God lives within you with the full confidence that your negatives can become positives. So you are to live with yourself with that same confidence that He will turn your negatives into positives.

You will begin to experience changes in your negative reactions only when you agree with God to do what is right, *now,* regardless of how you feel. Since you know what He expects of you, *step out and do it.* God gives the power to do His will. When in faith we join with God in choosing His will, we can be sure of the results!

\* \* \* \* \*

NOTE: For a more complete treatise of the subject of self-acceptance, see the author's book, *What Happens When You Meet You,* Living Life Publications, Drawer B, Montrose, Pennsylvania 18801

# Part II

## It's Not Good for Man to Be Alone

# 6

# Woman Was God's Idea—
# and He Had Reasons

Where there's a husband there's a woman.
Women! They've been:
    Worshipped — figuratively and literally.
    Respected.
    Loved.
    Fought over.
    Fought with.
    Praised.
    Extolled.
    Cursed.
    Blasphemed.
Men have died for them —
    Been murdered because of them.
    Lost their hearts to them.
    Sold their souls for them.
    Enslaved them.
    Treated them like queens.

Think of all the happiness they have brought into life, and all the sorrow, heartache, misery and suffering they have occasioned.

Did you ever catch yourself wondering, "Wasn't there a better way?"

The question and any answer you might give are academic, because — well — women *are* here. Men, women, and man-woman relationships are a part of the facts of life. So whether we like it or not; whether we can cope with it or not; women and men's involvement with them are inescapable realities.

Remember, women didn't just happen. They were God's idea. So if you're unhappy about life's arrangements, you'd better check with the Designer. Until you have, don't get too upset or blame women too much for who they are. After all they didn't ask to be around any more than you or I. What's more, they didn't ask to be *what* women are. God made them, and He did it after some rather extensive research. In other words, God had reasons for creating women, and for making her like she is. To understand a little about this we have to go back to the beginning.

> "And the Lord God formed man of the dust of the ground, and breathed into his nostrils the breath of life; and man became a living soul." Genesis 2:7

> "And the Lord God said, it is not good that the man should be alone; I will make him an help meet for him. And out of the ground the Lord God formed every beast of the field, and every bird of the heavens; and brought them unto the man to see what he would call them: and whatsoever the man called every living creature, that was the name thereof. And the man gave names to all cattle, and to the birds of

the heavens, and to every beast of the field; but for man
there was not found a help meet for him.

"And the Lord God caused a deep sleep to fall upon the
man, and he slept; and He took one of his ribs, and closed
up the flesh instead thereof; and the rib, which the Lord
God had taken from man, made he a woman, and brought
her unto the man. And the man said, this is now bone of my
bones, flesh of my flesh: she shall be called Woman, because
she was taken out of Man. Therefore shall a man leave his
father and mother, and shall cleave unto his wife: and they
shall be one flesh. And they were both naked, the man and
his wife, and were not ashamed."          Genesis 2:18–25

God saw it wasn't good for man to be alone. He not
only knew this, but he demonstrated it. Each of God's
creatures was brought to Adam to be named by him. This
meant Adam had understanding of the animal he was
naming but evidently there was no reciprocal communication of understanding. Not one species demonstrated the capability of being a help suited to Adam's
needs.

Why not?

Because there was no essential tie of relationship.
Physically there was commonality of origin — dust of the
earth. But apart from that there was no relationship of
nature. Each separate class of animals and man were a
distinct creation by God. In addition, man was made
from a different pattern, with an element in his being
beyond the physical. Man, though made from the dust,
was created in the image of God and became the recipi-
ent of God's gift of an immortal soul. In all the created
world, man stood unique and alone.

Imagine life with no one to share it! Even the Deity

enjoys the blessings of interaction and companionship through the Trinity. God the Father, God the Son, and God the Holy Spirit enjoy the blessedness of unbroken intimate fellowship. But it is not a fellowship between three Gods, rather the communion of three in one. One in nature or eternal, divine essence; yet three in separate personalities and functions. This is the mystery of the Godhead which goes beyond comprehension.

When God sought a help-mate suited to man's needs, He didn't create another person out of the dust. Instead He took a part of Adam and created woman, a being who was a part of Adam and yet different in personality and function. Woman as a part of man means man is incomplete without woman. Eve was the completion of Adam. Woman is the completion of man.

Since man was created in the image of God, it was necessary that the same essentials of the Godhead (in a very minute degree) exist in man. One of these essentials was that man be both a unit and a plurality — as is God. Man and woman are one in nature, of the same essence, and yet are two distinctly different persons in the expressions of their common being and in their function.

Yes, woman was God's idea — and He had reasons, profound and sacred reasons!

Is not the depth of our distortion expressed in the degree to which we are impatient with husband-wife differences, when we ought to be seeing the love and wisdom of God in those differences?

Take a minute and jot down some of the more obvious differences between you and your wife. Ron came up with a list about himself and Lois something like this:

| Lois | Ron |
|------|-----|
| Quick and spontaneous | Deliberate and slow |
| Verbal, easy talker | Man of few words |
| Excitable | Steady and calm |
| Intuitive | Logical |
| People centered | Work centered |
| Vivid | Prosaic |
| Gets up late, goes to bed late | Up early and to bed early |
| Hard to be on time | Always on time |
| Money is for pleasure | Money is for saving |
| Enjoys being loved, but not crazy about sex | Finds sex a release from tension |
| | Sexually aggressive |

The more Ron went over this list, the more he realized that the differences between him and Lois were really complimentary. For a long time they had seen them as competitive and the cause of friction between them. The idea that God had purposely made them different was a new and liberating thought. Looking at Lois and himself as people designed by God and purposely made different from each other gave him a new appreciation for both himself and his wife. Instead of allowing their differences to provoke conflict, he began to realize those same differences could be the ingredients for growth, harmony, and increasing happiness and usefulness as a couple.

After all, it's the contrasts in life that make it interesting and beautiful. Unbroken sameness wearies the spirit very quickly. Man was built to appreciate variety. You need to use this ability when variety is expressed in your own family!

What a change came into our own marriage when I began to recognize and accept our essential differences as gifts from God! Jill and I are *so* opposite that a Christian friend once told me: "Fred, even God couldn't bring harmony into your marriage. You and Jill are too different."

But God did! Not by remaking Jill, but by changing my viewpoint. That change began in the early years of our marriage, but it had to become a way of life. This took time.

Even today I find I can revert to the old way of thinking: "Why is Jill like that? Why isn't she different? That's not the way *I* would act!"

When I do revert to my old pattern, right away I'm frustrated and unhappy. Tension begins to build. I start feeling critical and resentful. Jill of course, doesn't change! But God isn't really trying to change her. He's trying to get me to change my negative attitude.

So he gently reminds me that Jill's essential personality pattern is just what I need, designed by Him for our mutual good. My job is to accept her differences as God's gifts and thank Him for them, because those differences are a necessary part of the whole Fred!

Do you grouse because your foot is different from your hands? Or complain because your ear is not like your eye? No, because each member of your body is a part of you!

God has not let me settle for anything less than the honest, practical realization and acceptance of my wife being a part of me.

Different? Yes.

Conflict and competition? Unnecessary!

I need her essentially *as she is* and she needs me essentially as I am. Here is the basis for both harmony and mutual freedom.

# 7

# She's Selfish Too!

"All have sinned and fall short of the glory of God."
Romans 3:23

God loving is the expression of His Glory.

A central quality of His love is His complete committal to the good of those He loves.

He is therefore continually "sitting where they sit," "feeling as they feel" and seeing life through their eyes and from their point of view.

There is no selfishness in God's love. This is why He can be completely objective and able to express His love without in the least compromising His justice.

Hell is an expression of the love of God. It shows us that He loves His universe too much to jeopardize the good of the many by refusing to deal in justice with the rebellious and incorrigible.

The heart of man's sin is his self-centeredness. Because of selfishness he continually falls short of God's glory which he was created to reveal. Even man's efforts to love are corrupted because he sees everybody and everything through the perspective of his own self-interest. This makes it impossible for a man to see his wife as she really is—as much in need of God's forgiveness and power to do what is right as he is.

Depravity (selfishness) is as real for her as it is for him. But just as it is difficult for us men to accept ourselves as we are with our selfish behavior, so it is equally difficult for us to accept our wives as they are with their self-centered behavior patterns.

Either we cling to the "ideal wife" image which was predominant in our minds when we fell in love and married, or else we are so hurt by the negatives in our wife which came to light after marriage that we can see nothing but evil in her.

Some men are afraid to let go of their unreal idealism because it would be too painful and shattering. Others react so strongly when the "real wife" comes to light that they allow cynicism or bitterness to distort their whole perspective. In either case they are unable to see their wives as they really are and accept them as actual persons who need (as we do) to be accepted, understood, encouraged and helped to grow.

When you fail to accept your wife as she is, you will either expect more than she can possibly give in your marriage, or you will reject her because you see her as completely negative. If you think of her as a negative person, then you will expect only negative reactions and performance from her. This will produce a chasm between you that will grow progressively wider. Where this happens, hope for a satisfying, stable marriage will turn into a fleeting mirage.

How different is God's love to us. He has no illusions about our negatives, yet He loves us just the same! He does not commit Himself in love to an ideal fantasy man, but to us just as we are, depraved yet redeemable sinners. He identifies with us in all our deep need for the sole purpose of leading us out of the quagmire of selfishness and onto the solid ground of redeemed living.

As a direct result of your experience of God's love to you there will be a new freedom in your relationship to God, to yourself, and to your wife. Likewise your wife will experience a new personal freedom toward herself and toward you. Her realization that *you accept her as she is* with a love that has her good at heart will set her free.

The candid recognition and acceptance of inborn selfishness in both ourselves *and our wives* are basic to a sound marriage relationship.

Dick was a quiet, idealistic, introverted and serious-minded college fellow. Having a good mind and above average general abilities, he was looked up to by his fellow students and appreciated by his professors, who saw in him potential for more than average usefulness. However few people knew his inner struggles and personal defeats which fed the fires of guilt and increased his feelings of inferiority and low self-esteem.

Dick found himself drawn to Lynne, a warm, outgoing, thoroughly dedicated Christian young lady, to whom he eventually became engaged. She drew the best out of him, challenged him to be his best for Christ, and was to a large degree responsible for his becoming a more balanced and inwardly free person. But the more Dick blossomed personally through Lynne's acceptance, admiration and love, the more he began to put her on a pedestal in his own mind.

As the pedestal got higher, Dick's love and admiration for Lynne began to be mixed with fear. What if she should discover the real, private, unknown-to-the-public Dick? At the heart of their love was a widening unrealism and idealism. In the wonder and delight of all the positives Dick felt in himself as a result of Lynne's love, he saw her *only as good*. His image of Lynne was unrealistic and distorted. In contrast, he saw himself as totally unworthy of this one who had pledged her heart and life to be his forever.

Little did Dick realize that Lynne too had secret struggles and defeats that made her afraid of being discovered, and caused her often to reject herself.

Strangely enough, while each admired the other, each was secretly afraid of the other.

For Dick and Lynne the path to reality was a long and tortuous one. It began on a trip during their engagement. On a long ride, in the hours of being together, they began to open their hearts and share their fears honestly with each other. To Dick's amazement he began to realize Lynne was human and weak. He had never thought of her as a real sinner, as much in need of the grace of God daily as he was. In the encouraging climate of Lynne's honesty, Dick too began to open up and venture to share just a bit of that which he had kept hidden. To his amazement and relief she did not reject him.

But this was only the start. The walls around personal seclusion were high. Dick's unrealistic image of Lynne went very deep. Much more than a few hours of intimate and honest sharing were needed to bring Dick to a wholesome objectivity in his image of Lynne. Again and again as their marriage progressed, Dick would be jolted by some manifestation in daily situations of the "unideal" Lynne. In resentment and disillusionment, he would cut her with those hurt-filled words:

"Why can't you be different?"

"How come you're this way?"

And the struggle within his own soul raged around the issue he'd faced only theoretically but not practically: God was calling him to love the Lynne that really was—not the Lynne he had imagined her to be.

Bit by bit they made the passage. Struggle and temptations to bitterness gave way to honest acceptance. As Dick grew in his awareness of *God's loving acceptance of him as he really was,* and experienced the liberation from fear and self-rejection that awareness of God's love brings, he found himself increasingly free and able to accept Lynne as a human being. Just as Dick had a nature that was inherently self-centered, which could only be good and right (self-giving) through moment by moment dependence on God's grace and power, the same was true for Lynne.

Today, as each prays and trusts God for the other, the earlier struggles and clashes that put strain in Dick's marriage are softening. He is maturing in his realization that acceptance of Lynne's selfishness as a part of her does not mean a passive putting up with it, nor even approval. Instead it elicits understanding and growing confidence that the mighty and loving Saviour who accepts both Dick and Lynne with their sin and selfishness will work an ongoing positive change in Lynne's life even as Dick expects that power to work effectively in his own life.

But the road to wholesome objectivity need not have been so long, the struggle so difficult, nor the risks so great. Many get lost along the way and are shipwrecked. Others stalemate and manage to endure without any progress. In those days Dick and Lynne found little help from the outside. They moved along by trial and error and not a few grief-filled times. You can shorten your path, lighten your load, reduce your struggles, and lessen your risks if you will begin today to reaffirm realistically:

1) Your whole-hearted acceptance of your wife as she is, including the fact that her self-centeredness is real.
2) That Christ is adequate for her selfishness just as truly as He is sufficient for yours.
3) That she will have the same difficulties experiencing Christ's victory over her selfishness as you have regarding yours.
4) That she is struggling with your selfishness just as you are with hers.
5) That your understanding of her, acceptance of her realities, and conscious trust in Christ *for her* are a vital key to her finding real answers for her own needs.
6) That as you pray faithfully and daily for her, and with real expectation that Christ will turn her negatives into positives, God will build increasingly in both of you the beauty of His personality.

# 8

# Your Wife Is Your Nearest Neighbor

"Thou shalt love thy neighbor as thyself."     Matthew 22:39

"Hi, Frank, what's the book today? Not that Bible again, I hope."

"Yep, it's that Bible again, Ted. In fact, it's the only book I carry with me to read a bit in spare minutes like lunch breaks."

"I don't know how you do it! It's enough for me to crack it once a week in church. Don't you find it awfully difficult and boring?"

"I'll admit to the difficult bit, Ted. There are some pretty big chunks in this old book I don't understand, but I really don't find it boring. And the more consistently I read it and think about what I've read the more interesting and exciting it becomes. Sometimes I stumble on something that seems simple and clear but as I mull it

65

over during work, a light turns on that suddenly makes some other parts of the Bible understandable."

"You mean, Frank, that you think about what you read after you've read it? Is that why you seem rather quiet when you're working? I've noticed you don't run off at the mouth like most of the guys around the place. I try to keep out of their cheap talk, but somehow I'm constantly drawn into it, and the first thing I know I've said things I wish I hadn't."

"I know what you mean, Ted. That used to be a real problem for me too. After I became a Christian I hated it even more. It seemed like every other word or phrase was a degrading remark about the most sacred and most intimate things in life — like God and sex. What was really tough was when the guys would make jokes about their bedroom experiences with their wives and talk about their private love-life like it was a common barnyard affair. It seemed like they were undressing their wives in public and making them cheap common property."

"Do you mean, Frank, that the cheap talk around here isn't a problem to you anymore?"

"No, I wouldn't say that, but it isn't nearly as much of a problem as it was. You see, I'm just not as aware of it as I was. I know the talk hasn't changed. If anything it seems to have gotten more free and even the secretaries get in on the act. But I don't think I hear it as much, or it rolls off more easily.

"Really, Ted, it's not that I'm any different from you or the guys. They don't enjoy their filthy talk any more than we do — that is, not in their better moments. When they go home to their wives, they can't help feeling like

they've betrayed them. You know, *one of the first steps toward unfaithfulness at home is for a fellow to lose respect for
himself."*

"How's that?"

"Well, if I've become cheap and small through acting
and talking like less than a man, I'm going to feel unworthy of the trust my wife has in me. And if I've bantered
about sex in such a way that has let the boys into our bed-
room, I've already subconsciously offered my wife to anyone who might be interested. When a person feels even
subconsciously that he's betrayed his wife and acted like a
beast, it's then a short and easy step to actual physical in-
fidelity."

"But how come you're not bothered like you say you
once were?"

"I guess it's a combination of things, Ted. One part is
this Bible I carry around. It used to be dull and terribly
difficult. So I read it only because I felt guilty if I didn't.
But something happened when Christ took over in my
life, and I began to feel like He was talking to me from
the Bible. It was still difficult and lots of it was boring, but
I began to stop getting hung up on those parts. Some of
it was alive and interesting, and many times very personal. Strangely enough, the more consistently I read it
the more interesting it became.

"But that wasn't all. God began to get very personal
with me. One day I was reading in the Old Testament
and the wickedness of using God's name in profanity hit
me. My swearing became increasingly wicked to me. I
began to see how unfaithful I was to God. While I never
dragged my wife and our sex life into our vulgar talk, in
effect I saw I treated God like some of the boys treated

67

their wives in their loose talk about them. My sin against God appeared to me far greater than their sin against their wives.

"In all of this I began to see why so many of us are either not Christians at all or weak half-hearted Christians at best. We allow our attitudes to God to become cheap, and by the same token He becomes cheap to us. This shows up in the careless, profane and insulting way we use God's name in our speech.

"No man can become greater than that which he worships. *The size of our God determines the size of our lives.*

"And you know, Ted, when I got thoroughly broken up over the way I had sinned against the almighty, eternal God, I began to have a new attitude toward what He says in the Bible. I found myself thinking about what I read. In fact I began to want to read more and to have time to mull it over in my mind. So really, I haven't needed to struggle against the sordid talk in the shop. My mind is so taken up with what I've read and its implications for life today that there's no room for the vulgar ideas floating all around me.

"Really Ted, it's great to be free from the double struggle. I don't have to fight to shut my ears to negative language, and I don't have to force myself to read the Bible. After all, we really don't mind doing what we enjoy, do we?"

"Thanks, Frank. What you've said really helps. I never thought of it that way. But could you explain a little more something you mentioned earlier?"

"Like what?"

"Well, you said sometimes a word or phrase hits you that seems to throw a flood of light on some part of the

Bible that's hard to understand. I don't quite get it. Do you mean that the Bible kind of explains itself?"

"Exactly. You know for years I had thought of the Bible as a huge book full of terrible no-no's — a bunch of do's and don'ts."

"Why of course, isn't that just what it is? A huge law book offering rewards to those who keep the rules and threatening horrible things to those who fail? I have a terrible time even remembering all the rules, much less trying to keep them."

"Ted, that's just what I used to think, and it tied me all in knots. But just recently I was reading about a discusssion Jesus was having with some lawyers. They were talking about this whole subject of rules. One of them asked Jesus which of the rules was the most important. Ted, His answer was fantastic. In effect, Jesus told the man there are only two rules!"

"Only two rules? What do you mean?"

"Well, here are His words . . ."

". . . Thou shalt love the Lord thy God with all thy heart, and with all thy soul, and with all thy mind. This is the first and great commandment. And a second like unto it is this. Thou shalt love thy neighbor as thyself. On these two commandments the whole law hangeth and the prophets."

Matthew 22:37–40

"You see, Jesus not only told the man which rules were most important, but He said every other rule in the book is rooted in just two basic laws."

"How can that be?"

"Well, this is what came as a flood of light to me. The whole Bible suddenly became easier to understand and

69

much more meaningful. What dawned on me is the fact that there are only two real relationships in life. A vertical one, man and God; and a horizontal one, man and his neighbor. And all the detailed laws in the Bible are but varied applications of these two great foundation rules."

"I never saw that before."

"But hang in there Ted. Even these two laws are just one."

"What do you mean by that?"

"Well, they are talking about just one thing — love, but love expressed in two directions. Since God is invisible, and my neighbor is very visible, tangible, and sometimes unpleasantly real, my love to God is measured by my demonstration of love to my neighbor.

"And do you know what Ted?"

"No, what?"

"My wife is my closest neighbor! The way I treat her is the tangible expression of how I relate to God."

"Hey Frank, come off it. Now you're getting to where it hurts, and I'm not sure I want to buy that idea."

"That's just the idea, Ted. Wham, this thought from Jesus' answer to the lawyer hits me — then my mind jumps to some other parts of the Bible like this one in I John 4:20:

> "If a man say, I love God, and hateth his brother, he is a liar: for he that loveth not his brother whom he hath seen, cannot love God whom he hath not seen."

"or this one in Roman 13:10:

> "Love worketh no ill to his neighbor: therefore love is the fulfillment of the law."

70

"And before you know it, God is talking to you all over the place. That's what I mean about the Bible becoming personal and meaningful. And believe me, when you get turned on and full of ideas like this, there's no room for all the stuff the guys in the shop seem to love to talk about. But you and I know they don't *really* love it. It's easy for the devil to fill an empty, idle mind, right?"

"You're too right, Frank. But back to this about a guy's wife being his closest neighbor and what that has to do with his relationship to God. I thought being a Christian and being a husband were two totally different things."

"In one way they are and in another way they're not. A man cannot be an adequate husband unless he is a real Christian. What a man is personally in himself as a Christian will inevitably be expressed by how he treats his wife. As I said before, my wife is my closest neighbor. She lives closer to me than anyone else does. A neighbor is as close to a person as their two lives interact. All other people can remain hidden to a degree within themselves and get along quite well with others. Most of us don't really know the people next door, yet we call them neighbors. But their real lives are hidden from us — and we don't try to pry into their private or personal affairs. A man's wife not only lives with him in the closeness of intimacy, but he sees much more of what she is really like than anyone else. So God commands him to love the real person (his wife) even as he comes to know her better and better.

"Since there are negatives in all of us, these negatives come to the fore along with the good traits. The problem we face in marriage is how to love what we don't like in our partners. How can a man love a person who has neg-

71

atives? It's easy to love the ideal, but we aren't married to ideals but to real people. In that sense every married person is living with his second spouse. We married an ideal and we're living with reality!

"But natural human love simply doesn't have what it takes to love raw human nature. That's why so many people reject themselves and others. The more a man sees his wife as she really is, the more impossible it is for him to love what he sees. In spite of all that may be said to the contrary, human nature, without the redemption of Jesus Christ is a sordid ugly thing. Look at these verses:

> "For from within, out of the heart of men, evil thoughts proceed, fornication, theft, murders, adulteries, covetings, wickedness, deceit, lasciviousness, an evil eye, railing, pride, foolishness:"                                     Mark 7:21,22

> "For the flesh lusteth against the Spirit, and the Spirit against the flesh; and these are contrary the one to the other; that ye may not do the things that ye would. But if ye are led by the Spirit, ye are not under the law. Now the works of the flesh are manifest, which are these: fornication, uncleanness, lasciviousness . . ."     Galatians 5:17–21

"Since my human nature is just as full of negatives as my wife's, our increasing closeness can only bring clashes and tension. Without a work of God in us, we bring out the worst in each other. You don't have to read the papers or look into many homes to see what I've just said amply demonstrated every day.

"That's why a man can't be what he should be as a husband unless he is a real Christian. He doesn't have the resources within himself. He can have the needed resources only as they come to him from Christ and as he trusts Christ for them. Only God's love can love the twisted and sordid in human nature. In the degree to which *God's love is real* in a man's heart will he find himself loving his wife as she really is. What's more, this kind of love, originating in God has a wonderful quality about it. Instead of stimulating the negatives in another, it subdues them. It has a redemptive influence on those who are its objects. It heals instead of hurts, builds instead of destroys, strengthens instead of weakens. This is part of the meaning in Ephesians 5:25:

> "Husbands, love your wives, even as Christ also loved the church, and gave himself for it."

"Since, in relating to his wife, a man is relating to real life, his family relationship is the expression of the reality of his Christianity.

"No man is more a Christian than what he lives in his own home!"

"Frank, you've surely given me a lot to think about. Thanks."

\* \* \* \* \*

The discussion between Frank and Ted touched some of the heart issues in family relationships. Central to those issues is the question of God and His presence in the very heart of a man's life. Since God is love, a man must have God as a living, experiential reality living within him if he is going to love his wife as he loves himself. In fact, without God's love within he can't even take the first step of loving himself properly, much less love the woman to whom he is committed.

Perhaps you should stop right here and ask yourself some honest questions:

Are you really a Christian?

When and how did you become one?

Are you learning to walk and live as a Christian?

I became a Christian as a teen-age farm boy. It happened one night when I was alone, doing chores. I was miserable with guilt and felt completely helpless about my youthful sinfulness. Suddenly the thought crossed my mind that Jesus loved me — just as I was, even in all my naughtiness. The thought persisted and intensified. It was so personal and so real, there was only one thing to do and I did it. Right there beside the barn I got down on my knees and thanked Jesus Christ for loving me and for dying for me. That's when I became a Christian.

It took years before I realized that one lives as a Christian by exactly the same process involved in becoming a Christian — . As Paul put it in Colossians 2:6:

> "As therefore you received Christ Jesus the Lord, so walk in Him." — (by trusting)

Becoming a Christian is like the first step in a long journey. Traveling the journey is but a continuous succession of steps, each like the original!

What was my first, original step? Turning from myself with my sin and guilt to acceptance of Christ's love, forgiveness and acceptance of me.

My Christian life has been a series of such steps — developing into a way of life. At every place where I have become conscious of sin, inadequacy or need, I have found the answer only by a fresh acceptance of Christ's love, forgiveness and acceptance.

74

Increasingly I have become free to be myself, free to serve God without fear of failure, and free from frustrating and disappointing struggles for victory and inner peace. This is how God meant us to live as Christians.

The thrilling part is how it has affected our home! Finding Christ's love adequate for myself has resulted in me setting Jill and my children free to find Christ adequate for themselves. My faith in Christ for them is also more real, because it springs from a growing reality in my own experience. I know they need Him daily and just as much as I do. But I also know He loves them *as they are* just as He loves me *as I am.*

Why not settle the issue, if you are not sure you are a Christian?

Ask Christ to come in and take over all of your life, the good and the bad.

Then take another step and thank Jesus Christ that He loves both you *and* your wife *as you are.* Choose *now* to rejoice in His love for her as well as for you.

# Part III

Life Takes a Heap of Living

# 9

# The One Who Leads Is the Leader

"Give me a man to surrender to and I'll eat out of his hand," exploded Debby, "but you've got to be that man!"

Her remark cut Brent to the quick, because deep within he knew he should "be that man" and provide the leadership his wife inwardly wanted but outwardly resisted.

"I may be a shrew, but it's up to you to do the taming," Debby added.

This just drove the knife deeper into Brent's conscience. He was afraid of Debby, and he knew she knew it. He was weak, timid, insecure, and indecisive. When faced with decisions he was hesitant, unsure, and in that moment of vacillation Debby would either make the decision or impatiently remark,

"Well, hurry up. Make up your mind. We haven't got all day!"

Deep within, Brent wanted Debby to make the decisions, then he would have her to blame if they were wrong. He was afraid of the responsibility involved in leadership.

To make matters worse he confused love toward his wife with pleasant peaceful feelings between them and so Brent felt he should pay almost any price to keep the peace in his home. This resulted in giving in to Debby's desires even against his better judgment. He didn't realize that love involves firmness and making decisions that might leave his wife unhappy!

Brent and Debby traveled a rough road in the early days of their marriage. With Brent's fear of leadership, coupled with a false concept of love, he was completely confused as to what their problem really was. Time made the situation worse. Not knowing how to work toward a solution, the problem became more complicated.

Occasionally Brent would rise up and really lay down the law to his wife. But her resistance frustrated him and stimulated harsh words with bitter feelings, then when the issue cooled Brent would be deeply convicted for being an unloving husband. He could find no peace until he had gone to Debby and asked her forgiveness. Often her response was scorn and resentment.

"I don't want your apologies, I want you to be different," she flung at him one day.

Once again Brent crawled back into his miserable shell, totally frustrated by this quick, sharp and seemingly unconquerable wife that he was married to — "until death us do part." Deep within he knew the fault was his, even though all his friends sympathized with him and blamed Debby for her lack of submission to her husband.

* * * * *

Way back in the Garden of Eden man copped out on true leadership. When Eve was tricked by the serpent and ate the forbidden fruit, Adam relinquished his leadership by saying: "have it your way dear, and I'll join you. . ."

Instead of holding true to God, he turned from loyalty to God to being loyal to his wife, her interests and the pleasantness of happy feelings between them. What he should have done at that crisis moment was expect Eve to repent, and taking her to God, insist she get right with Him against whom she had sinned.

## TRUE LEADERSHIP

Leadership is committed to promoting the best interests of those who are led. There is no room for selfishness in true leadership. *It is the farthest thing from dictatorship.* A dictator is interested only in *his* goals and *at the center of his goals is himself.* He may do many good things for others, but behind all he does are his own interests. When the crunch comes he is prepared to sacrifice even his friends in order to achieve his goals.

True leadership cannot be divorced from true love. They are part of each other. A leader in this sense *is prepared to sacrifice himself for the sake of those he leads.*

Jesus Christ is the truest leader. He loves perfectly and at the same time He commands completely. In effect He says, "Follow me and I will do you good." And to effect that good for us, He gave His life!

That's why it's perfectly safe to surrender implicitly to His Lordship. Both our fullest security and our highest good inevitably result from capitulation to His leadership.

Jesus Christ has made it vividly clear that His love and authoritative leadership work for our eternal blessing. In a similar though much more limited way, Adam's leadership of Eve was to bring blessing to her; and our wives are to be better people because of our loving leadership of them. This is so clearly stated in Ephesians 5:25:

> "Husbands, love your wives, even as Christ also loved the church, and gave himself for it."

God created woman with an inner demand for leadership. Her whole nature cries out for it. She wants strength to surrender to, and love in that strength to make her surrender a safe experience. "Faint heart never won fair maiden" is true because woman's nature doesn't dare surrender to weakness. Where she sees weakness in her husband a woman will not and cannot surrender. She despises weakness in men, and most of all in the man to whom she is married.

The heart of *family* weakness is rooted in the husband's failure and/or refusal to provide the leadership of love that God designed woman's nature to respond to. We have opted for being good providers, rather than true leaders. A leader does provide for those he leads, but provision of their material needs is not leadership!

In the measure that a husband fails to lead, his wife automatically takes over. The very strength in her which he fears is like the steel against which steel is sharpened. If a man only realized it, the strength of his wife is designed by God to make him a stronger, better man — a godly leader.

## BECOMING THE LEADER IN YOUR HOME

"Fred, do you realize you are not fit to be married to a woman until you know first what it means to be married to Jesus Christ?"

This disturbing statement by a close friend stuck with me all during the three years of my engagement to Jill. While I believed those words theoretically, the real truth behind them did not hit me until after we were married.

In the early months of our marriage we were much like Brent and Debby. Like Brent I was insecure, fearful, and mixed up about what it meant to be a loving leader in my home. Jill was strong, expressive, and obviously very frustrated by my indecision and lack of leadership. But the problem was deeper than my failure to lead. I did not realize that love was more than good feelings!

I wanted a happy home where pleasant feelings ruled. But when conflicts arose between us, I would get convicted for being unloving and apologetically revert to passive indecision.

At a critical point in our conflict another friend repeated the same truth I had been told years before. The words were different but they expressed the same basic reality.

I was sharing a little about my struggle to be the loving husband I felt God wanted me to be. My friend's question came like a shaft of light in the darkness:

"Fred, in your relationship with your wife are you being loving toward her or loving toward the commandments of God?"

He went on to explain that the *foundation* for a husband's leadership is his total submission to the authority and commandments of God. God's will was to have the first claim in his life. It was to come before his concern for his wife's or his own interests or feelings.

This means that leadership is rooted in the leader's own submission to a higher authority; an authority that commands his commitment to that which is right, appropriate or best for *all* concerned — for those he leads as well as for himself as leader.

For many couples there is a nagging feeling that selfishness is the real reason for their conflicts. Usually each accuses his spouse of being selfish inwardly even if not outwardly. Then his own conscience also subtly suggests that he is being selfish.

It is difficult, if not impossible for genuine harmony to exist when one feels the other person is after something for himself at his partner's expense. This is particularly true in relationship to the role and operation of leadership.

To function effectively as leader in your home, your spirit and conscience must be free even from subtle forms of self-seeking. This can become increasingly real as you honestly, consistently, and repeatedly choose to base your decisions on what you understand to be God's will, rather than your own or your wife's purely personal desires. Remember God's will is always the best for *all* concerned. It is *always* appropriate to any given situation.

As you become increasingly free in yourself to submit to God's desires for you and your family, several results will begin to emerge:

1. You will become more relaxed, free, and inwardly secure.

2. You will become more objective as you seek answers to areas of family conflict.
3. Your wife and children will sense that you are submitted to God's authority; that your position as leader in your home is clearly *not* that of an autocrat making arbitrary decisions. Even though they may resist your leadership, their conscience will affirm that your motives are right.
4. God will work even in unseen ways to support your leadership while you are committed to that which *He wants* for your family. Therefore you will not have to "fight for your leadership rights."
5. As you demonstrate clear God-centered motives and exercise God-supported authority, the Holy Spirit will begin teaching you the *spirit* of leadership. It is love with a deeper dimension. Love that is concerned with the well-being of those loved including yourself! From this foundation will spring wholesome happy feelings and the emotional satisfactions that are so vital to effective family living.

## THE WORK OF LEADING

Leading is work. Being "king of your castle" may boost your ego, but unless there is more to your leadership than status, your crown is already slipping.

To be the leader in your home you will have to work consistently toward the realization of three objectives:

1. To know each member of your family, beginning with your wife.
2. To encourage the development and use of the gifts God has given each member of your family.
3. To pace yourself as leader to the capacity of those you lead.

Remember the *ultimate objective* in family leadership is the securing of the highest good for the total family. Therefore you need to make it your business to know those you seek to lead. This is a part of what Peter means in I Peter 3:7:

> "Husbands, dwell with your wives according to knowledge. . ."

How well do you know your wife? Each child?

Are you alert, interested in things that interest them?

What are their strengths? Weaknesses? Needs?

Is communication open? Free? Lovingly honest?

How well do you understand one another? Does your wife rate you as an understanding husband?

To get to know your wife involves spending time with her, sharing yourself and your heart with her, and making it easy for her to share herself with you. The same is true for your children.

There are no set rules for achieving understanding except *to work at it* lovingly, patiently and persistently. For some it will be an exciting adventure with understanding blossoming as a flower opening to the sun. For others there will be struggle, discouragement, and the need for patient plodding. Very few homes will have genuine understanding without working at it.

The second objective is to encourage the development and use of the gifts God has given each member of your family.

> One day God seemed to be saying to me, "Fred, you're the head of your home?"

"Yes."

"Have you ever thought that you are responsible for the development of Jill's gifts?" What will you have to show when I call you for an accounting of your stewardship of the gifts I gave her?"

"What do you mean by that?"

"I mean that I gave Jill some gifts. These are to be developed and used for My glory. As her leader, you have been entrusted with the stewardship of those gifts. And one day I'll ask you to give an accounting of how you encouraged Jill to use them.

"But Lord, I thought Jill's place was in the home, to do the things I want done."

And so the "conversation" went, until I was jolted into another dimension of my leadership as God sees it. He began to tell me that He really wasn't too interested in my personal ideas of family. Instead He was very concerned that the gifts He had put in both Jill and me should be developed and used.

I got the message. God hadn't given me my lovely and gifted wife just for my personal pleasure and benefit. Rather she was mine to be a part of the fulfillment of God's purposes for both of us. His plan was that our mutual gifts should work together for achieving common God-given objectives.

Before that experience I was mainly concerned about *my* career. Jill's role in the home was taken for granted. She was supposed to fit the generally accepted pattern for wives of Christian workers. This involved being my wife, a mother, and a home-maker. Of course she should be a

Christian witness by her life. Then in some non-defined way she was to assist in my ministry. I had never really thought about *her* God-given gifts and how they were to fit into the overall pattern of our lives.

God made it plain that I was accountable for the use of what He had given her!

This experience was a turning point in our home. I saw the validity of it all. I realized that a leader's real strength lies in the total resources of those he leads, and it is his responsibility to discover and utilize those resources.

To meet the issue we had to do some honest evaluating, earnest praying and creative thinking. Since Jill's gifts are ministry-directed, we had to ask ourselves how and in what ways she could be active in a ministry without conflicting with the priorities of being a wife and mother.

God hadn't suggested that her normal roles at home be set aside. The Bible makes it clear that wifehood and motherhood are God-given privileges and responsibilities. But we were to see them as part of a larger picture, where the totality of my wife's personality and God-given abilities should blossom into usefulness.

I had been content to let Jill fit the stereotype. It was easy and rather flattering to think of her role as my "servant," given by God to please and satisfy my desires! It hadn't occurred to me that there might be ways she could discharge her normal responsibilities and at the same time develop and use her non-domestic gifts.

At that time our children were still young. She had the burden of a large old home, four growing children and two adults. The physical load itself was about all Jill could handle. Unknown to me, Jill had been praying that

God would show us how she could find relief from the physical burden of laundry, cleaning, and household chores, and be given time and strength for the ministry that was on her heart.

One day a letter came with a specific request: "Please use the enclosed check to pay for some household help."

This was the beginning of the answer. God directed us to a consecrated Christian lady who became Jill's part-time helper in our home. This released Jill for time to study and prepare for a ministry to women. Having someone else clean, wash, iron, and do the dishes didn't make her any less a wife and mother. But she now had time and strength to use her ministry gifts.

She began in a limited way by teaching "Mother's Clubs" in our own home after the small children were in bed. In time her ministry grew into a varied outreach to women. But it was always kept compatible with the changing needs of a growing family and the particular demands of my own life-work.

For this to develop as it did required leadership on my part, open and honest communication between Jill and me, and the constant submission of purely personal desires to what both of us felt was the will of God for that particular time. Underneath was a oneness of spirit between us that God developed through the years, which now bore fruit in a satisfying and exciting life for all the family.

People are different. Each person is an individual and each family is unique in its combination of responsibilities, God-given gifts and opportunities. Speaking and Bible teaching are not the only gifts God gives! Perhaps your wife has a gift for entertaining, being a peace-maker or is creative with her hands. Your job as leader in your home is to discover *in companionship with your wife* what God's way is for you and your family at any particular stage of the family's development. Don't settle for the easy path of stereotyped living. At the same time don't fall into the trap of looking for something exciting for excitement's sake.

What God has for you will be *appropriate* to your whole family, with its needs, its gifts and its abilities. But to discover His way will require openness, communication, innovative thinking, believing prayer, and the willingness to take steps of obedience to whatever God may say to your heart.

To you whose children are in school, away at college, or even completely out of the nest: remember, your wife has more servants at her command than kings and queens had in a past age. Modern technology has removed many of the physical burdens of life. How is your wife to use her time, if you insist that "a woman's place is in the home?"

The third objective toward which you as leader will have to work is to pace yourself as leader to the capacity of those you lead.

When I was single I was free to be and do pretty much what I liked within the bounds of propriety and my personal resources. I hitch-hiked around the country, kept my own hours, and spent my money as I liked. All that changed when I acquired a wife. Additional restrictions were ours when our first baby was born. Travel became much more complicated with each additional member of our family!

The leader of any team is automatically restricted by

the pace at which those led are able or willing to follow! While we accept this in industry, business, and the world of sports, we seem to ignore it in the family.

One major cause for tension in the home is the *individualism* that persists in family life even though it may have been subordinated in other areas of life. A corporate executive knows and accepts the fact that he cannot move faster than his management team. But the same successful executive may fail miserably at home. Why?

Because he doesn't see his family, and particularly his wife, as a part of himself. At home he thinks as a rugged individualist. At the office he operates as part of a corporate whole. Such a person is actually more married to his job than he is to his family!

Did you ever see one foot walking faster than the other could follow? A friend had severe arthritis in one hip which affected the ability of one leg to function normally. His walk automatically slowed to the capability of the weak leg. In his case, he accepted his condition and learned to live with it. I never saw him angry or resentful because one leg restricted his mobility.

Have you really identified with your wife and children in terms of their capability?

Scott had served a term as a single missionary in a remote area among primitive people. He loved it and became devoted to the people. When he came home for an extended furlough, he married and became a father. Later, when Sherry was pregnant with their second child, they returned to the field.

Sherry was an intelligent, attractive and dedicated girl who had never been overseas before. Going to a remote village

91

to live among primitive people was both new and frightening to her. Being pregnant didn't help.

Scott was totally unaware of Sherry's fears. He was eager to get back among the people he loved, to identify with them, to learn their language and give them parts of the Bible in their own dialect. Primitive living conditions didn't bother Scott. He had learned to see past the lack of sanitation, strange food and ever present diseases so common to those people.

Even before they arrived on the field Scott was psychologically buried in his exciting work. He was completely oblivious to the danger signals being flashed by Sherry. She felt alone, deserted. Communication had never been too good between them, but now when she desperately needed his understanding and strength, he just wasn't there. In heart he was identified with "his" people and "his" work. Although physically present, in spirit he was unaware of his wife as a person in deep need.

Not long after they arrived on the field, Sherry froze psychologically and had to be flown out of the jungle on emergency leave. Her problem was intensified by nagging guilt:

> "If I can't take it, Scott won't be able to continue, and I'll be responsible for the damnation of all the heathen who would have been saved had Scott been able to stay."

Scott sought help and happily was shown that his failure to pace himself to Sherry's capacity was the real problem. He responded positively and began to think of Sherry as his other self, to identify with her and her needs and to provide those complimentary strengths that her nature required.

You can't lead your family faster than they are willing or able to follow. How can you tell you are not running too far ahead? What are the evidences that you have set for them a reasonable and comfortable pace?

If you should ask your wife about this aspect of your leadership, and if she were free to answer honestly, what would she say?

Why not make the subject of leadership a topic for an after dinner conference? If not that, then at least discuss it periodically with your wife.

# 10

# Love Costs—and You Can't Pay It

"Husbands, love your wives . . .
  As Christ also loved the church . . .
    And gave Himself up for it . . .
      That He might" . . . do something . . .
        Wonderful for it . . .
                              Ephesians 5:25 ff

Love is self-giving.

Love is purposeful.

Love is redemptive — i.e., the other person is better because of my love.

Love is the committal of the will to the promotion of the well-being of the person loved. At its heart is self-giving — for the other's good. This is the way God loves, and it cost Him His life!

Genuine self-giving is foreign to man. The deep underlying drive in man is getting, not giving. When he does give, it is usually to get something.

Why did you get married?

Take a sheet of paper and pencil and jot down five reasons why you got married. Would the sheet look something like this?

I couldn't live without her.

I was lonely, and she warmed my heart.

Every time I looked at her she turned me on. She was for me.

She was great to be with, and I decided I wanted it to be permanent.

I needed a companion.

Do you see a common denominator running through each statement? Getting!

Most people marry in order to get something. I can't remember talking to anyone who said: "I just had to spend my life making that girl happy, so we got married."

Of course we know marriage will cost. But we tend to think of cost more in terms of the physical. Like:

It will cost me some freedom.

There will be bills to pay.

I'll have to adjust a bit to her way of thinking and living.

I'll have to be careful about friendships with other women.

Will she be upset with me when I have to travel for the boss?

Can I earn enough to keep her happy?

I want kids, but does she?

I'll have to put up with her family and friends.

Will she resent my times with the boys, especially during hunting season?

Few of us think of cost in terms of the deeper element of true self-giving for the good of the other. It's when marriage makes demands on our own self-interest that trouble starts. Most marriage problems are rooted in one simple fact: selfishness.

"But this shouldn't be a problem for Christians."

Maybe it shouldn't be, but it is.

Take some time to think about your marriage frictions. Use paper and pencil. Jot down every instance of tension, inner frustration, hurt, argument, or whatever came between you and your wife that you can remember during the last week or so.

In which of these did someone's selfishness play a major part?

How many of these were caused by love?

How many of those unpleasant experiences would have been avoided if your objective in marriage was to make your wife a better person through your love?

BEING A CHRISTIAN DOESN'T AUTOMATICALLY SOLVE THE SELFISHNESS FACTOR!

This can be solved ONLY in the degree to which the Christian dies to selfishness, for LOVE and SELFISHNESS CANNOT COEXIST.

## WHAT IS LOVE?

Much friction in marriage is rooted in our confused idea of what real love is. We tend to think of love, especially married love, as a feeling. Love is deeper than emotion, even though emotion is a part of love.

Love is first an act and a set of the will. Emotion, or feeling, is one expression of love. We put most of the emphasis on the feeling aspect of love. But we know little about *choosing* to love.

WE *CAN* CHOOSE TO LOVE!

If this were not true, God could not command us to love. But He does. He *commands* us to:

> Love God — "Thou shalt love the Lord thy God with all thy heart, and with all thy soul, and with all thy mind . . ."
> Matthew 22:37

> Love the Lord Jesus — "If any man love not the Lord Jesus Christ, let him be accursed."     I Corinthians 16:22

> Love our neighbors — "Thou shalt love thy neighbor as thyself."     Matthew 22:39

> Love our wives—"Husbands, love your wives, even as Christ also loved the church, and gave Himself up for it;"
> Ephesians 5:25

> Love husbands and children — "That they (older women) may train the young women to love their husbands, to love their children . . ."
> Titus 2:4 (So we can be trained to love)

Because love is rooted in an attitude of the will, we do not need to be the helpless victims of our emotions or feelings! Emotions fluctuate. They are stimulated by a wide variety of factors, many of them totally unpredictable and often unexplainable. Because we tend to make emotion and love synonymous, we have a hard time figuring out the difference between true love and excited feelings.

A man may become emotionally cold to his wife, and then "fall in love" with another woman. Since we can choose to love, we can also choose not to yield to feelings of interest in an illegitimate object! More about that later.

When our first parents declared their independence

97

of God and turned to live for what they wanted instead of what God wanted, something happened to their love for each other.

One of the beautiful elements in the first home was the total self-giving love that bound Adam and Eve together. Each thought of the other as a part of himself. Adam said of Eve: "She is bone of my bones and flesh of my flesh . . . ," i.e., "She is part of me!" They talked "we" language. The simple fact is that no man really hates his own flesh. He cares for it, and if a part of him gets hurt, he nurses and takes care of the hurt part of him rather than swearing at it and rejecting it.

But when sin came into the lives of Adam and Eve, immediately there was a change in their love. Instead of oneness, an awareness of separateness came over them. Adam told God, "The woman you gave me is responsible for our disobedience . . ." He began to talk the language of "him" and "her" instead of "us" and "we." He no longer saw Eve as part of himself, but as a separate person. SELFISHNESS HAD CORRUPTED THEIR LOVE. The element of "getting" replaced the element of "giving."

All natural human love is now rooted in and expressed through man's deep-seated native selfishness. It takes the miracle of God's redeeming power to change love from being self-centered to self-giving.

The identification of love with feelings or emotions is one evidence of the fatal distortion that corrupts human love. Haven't you heard this sort of comment:

> "I don't love my wife any more, so I guess there's nothing left for me to do but call it quits."

\* \* \* \* \*

"After all, if they don't love each other any more, you can't expect them to keep on living together."

\* \* \* \* \*

"Isn't it wonderful how happy Joe is with his new bride. He really seems to be in love. You know, he told me the other day he only thought he was in love with his first wife. When he found out it wasn't the real thing they divorced. It's sure too bad. She seemed like a really good woman, and now she's got to rear the children alone. And of course Joe has the burden of their support along with the care of the new home and his new wife. But since he really loves his new bride, I guess it will go O.K. In any case, I hope for everyone's sake that this marriage is for real."

\* \* \* \* \*

Marc and Bev came to see me one day. They had been married for many years and the children were nearly grown. Marc summarized their situation:

"I never did really love my wife, and I just figured it was not right to keep on living a lie. I feel that we as Christians ought to be honest and live honestly. So, when I met and fell in love with Sandy I knew she was the one for me. Bev wouldn't give me a divorce, so I started going with Sandy openly. Now she is carrying my child. What I want is to marry the girl I love and be finished with this sham sort of living."

This is just how selfish love (which is natural to all of us) may be expected to operate. Being centered in self-interest, and concerned with "*getting*" instead of "*giving*," as soon as the "getting" stops, the "love" ceases. Marc really was saying:

"Bev doesn't stimulate loving feelings in me any more, so I am justified in considering divorce. Even though she won't

99

give it to me, I've got to live with the woman who gives me the pleasant feelings that I know are true love."

Increasingly the literature dealing with love, courtship, and marriage and/or the subject of divorce is committed to this basic concept that love is emotion. When the emotion is gone between partners we are told there is nothing wrong with responding to some other person who stimulates that emotion we call "love."

God's love, and the love He develops in us through Redemption is entirely different. It consists in giving of one's self for the good of the one loved. It is rooted in a committal of the will. Of course there are emotions. They are an expression of love, not its foundation. God finds delight and joy in giving Himself for the blessing of others. The happiness He feels is not love, it is the *product of love*. He does not love us because it makes Him happy to do so. He loves us so that we may be happy. His good feelings arise as a result of the blessings His love brings in our lives.

"God so loved the world that He gave His only begotten son . . ."

God's love cost — Himself. And all love will cost — ourselves. Because God chooses to love in this way — self-giving — He is able to love those in whom there is no response. Because His love has as its goal our good and happiness, He can love those who are in themselves unlovely. It is this self-giving, consistent, purposeful love in God and expressed toward us which breaks our resistance and brings about in us a love-response to God.

In the same way, when a man is touched in his heart by the love of God, and when he commits himself by an act of his will to promote the well being of his wife, he has established a solid foundation upon which a lasting, satisfying marriage can be built. The stability of his marriage will not be threatened by the fickle nature of human emotion, nor will it be threatened by that which he finds unlovely in his wife.

God doesn't love us because we are lovely. *He loves us because He wants to do us good.*

You and I are to love our wives in the same way, *not in proportion to their being lovable,* but because we choose to do them good.

In the Bible, love is always described in terms of attitude and activities, not in terms of feelings. The famous love-chapter, I Corinthians 13:4–8, describes love this way:

| *What love does do* | *What love does not do* |
|---|---|
| Love is patient. | Love does not envy. |
| Love is kind. | Love does not push itself forward. |
| Love suffers long and is kind. (while it suffers) | Love does not boast. |
| Love is glad with the truth. | Love does not act inappropriately. |
| Love is protective. | Love does not act selfishly. |
| | Love does not get huffy. |
| | Love does not keep a record of the other person's wrongs. |
| | Love does not exult in evil. |

In Romans 13:10 we are told: "Love works no hurt to his neighbor." Your wife is your closest neighbor!

What if your wife doesn't respond to this kind of love?

What if she keeps on being nastily selfish?

Do you *have* to keep on loving a woman who seems to choose being unlovely and making life miserable for you?

You don't *have* to do anything!

But if your heart is full of God's love, then you *want* to do what love does — keeps on loving!

Our problem is we are constantly leaving God out of the picture. Just as you need God's love in order really to love your wife *regardless,* so God must work in *her* heart a response to you that comes from God. Remember our chapter about depravity being a reality? Read it again. Every selfish heart needs Jesus Christ. True love is impossible while the heart is selfish, and without Christ your wife is incapable of responding in love to you *no matter how consistently you love her.*

This is where faithful believing prayer comes in. Your love alone will not of itself guarantee that your wife will change. *Please don't start loving with her change as your goal.*

She might not change!

But God's love in you must go on loving!

*Your faith must be in God,* that He will change her — *not* in your love, that it will change her. Keep God-centered in your thoughts. Keep your faith regarding your wife God-centered, and you will be preserved from temptations to bitterness should the answer seem like a long time coming.

During a visit to Africa I spoke to a group who met

in the home of an African Christian. This man had an unusual reputation for godliness in the town where he lived. After the meeting he showed me a picture of an African woman dressed in wedding attire.

"This is a picture of my dear wife," he said. "She's not saved yet, but Jesus satisfies me."

Later I heard the story. Twelve years earlier, Samuel had been wonderfully converted. With his heart full of a new God-given love he became a completely new kind of husband. Instead of a harsh, demanding, self-centered man that was typical of the nominal Christians and pagan Africans around him, Samuel began to treat his wife as one whom he truly loved. He began to demonstrate I Corinthians chapter 13 in his home and family life. Instead of being a dictator he became a leader who was loving, thoughtful, considerate and helpful.

But Miriam rejected both her husband and his God. She despised Samuel. Instead of responding to his love, she hardened her heart, and seemed to do everything in her power to make life unbearable for him. She began to run with other men in the town. When she would come home she would taunt her husband, curse him, and flaunt herself toward him but refuse to allow him to touch her.

To most men Miriam would have been impossible. But Samuel kept on loving, and after twelve years of this ordeal he still spoke of her with tenderness . . . "This is my *dear* wife. She's not saved yet."

How did he do it?

He kept his heart right with God day by day, as expressed by his statement, "Jesus satisfies me."

Secondly he kept his faith steady by consistently believing his wife would be saved, even though he saw no probability of it happening. In the interim he kept on trusting God and being loving.

Several years later an African friend from those parts was traveling in the U.S. After a meeting where he spoke, I asked about Samuel's wife.

"Was she ever converted?"

"Oh yes, hadn't you heard?" replied my friend. "She was gloriously saved not long after your visit. We weren't really surprised. How could she resist the love of Christ that her husband demonstrated day by day? She would get into some awful scrapes, and in desperation would turn to her husband for help. He always had that same tender and loving reply:

"Here is some help for you dear. I'm sorry to hear of your trouble. You know, don't you that all I have is yours. I'm keeping it just for you, because I love you so."

"She finally broke," continued my friend, "and now they are living happily together, a wonderful example of the triumphant power of the love of Christ in the heart of a man."

Yes, love costs — but neither you nor I can pay it. Only Christ in us can. If you can't love your wife for her own sake, then love her for Christ's sake. You and I need to get on with the loving — and leave in God's mighty hands the matter of our wife's responding.

## HOW TO BUILD LOVE

The love we've just described doesn't usually "happen" in a flash of spiritual ecstasy. For most of us it must be built — and building involves steps — and time — and perseverance. However, before you read any further, ask yourself:

"Do I really *need* a different quality of love?"

You won't attempt seriously to build what you aren't convinced you need. It costs too much. But if you really want to have a different quality of love for your wife, here are some practical steps which will help.

1. To what degree are you committed consciously to do good to your wife?

   List on paper some of the things you do which indicate to you that you are really committed to doing good to her.

2. Be sure you have accepted yourself as a person who is accepted by God.

   Your attitude to others is often a projection of your attitude toward yourself. If you cannot love yourself, you probably cannot love your wife. Go back to Part I, Chapter 5 and re-read it carefully.

   God loves you as you are, not as you ought to be or as you would be if you had made better choices along the way. Since God loves you as you are, you have to love yourself as you are. You dare not reject the "you" God has accepted, or hate the "you" whom He loves.

   You must be very honest with yourself and with God at this point. When you can wholeheartedly rest in the fact that God has taken over the full responsibility for dealing with your negatives, then you can be free about the real person your wife is. It is the *real* woman you've chosen to love — not the woman she would be if she'd change in some ways.

105

Take just a minute now and demonstrate your acceptance of yourself by telling God audibly you thank Him for accepting and loving you!

Tell Him further you accept yourself and you thank Him for yourself.

Tell Him you praise Him for loving you as you are, and therefore you choose to love yourself as you are.

Thank Him that He knows all about your weaknesses and sins, and you are glad He is working right now to save you from them.

Take some time each morning for a whole week to do this. Get alone, in your basement or car or someplace where you can talk to God aloud about these things.

3. Accept your wife as God's gift to you and do this by a definite, deliberate act of your will. Periodically review this acceptance by consciously *thanking God* that He *gave* your wife to you. Your attitude toward a gift usually is determined by who the giver is!

4. Accept your children as God's gifts to you. Name each one, and be very sure you choose to thank God in a special way for that child who may be more of a trial to you than the others.

5. Make a list on paper of the positive qualities in your wife, then in each of your children. Go over the list and deliberately thank God for each one of the items.

There is something positive about every person. In addition, there is almost unlimited potential for good in every person. Thank God for these also.

If you can't see any positive qualities in one member of your family, then concentrate on thanking God for the *potential* for good in that person!

106

Remember — God is committed to this fact: MAN IS RE-DEEMABLE!

6. This step is especially important, but you *dare not* take it until after you have completed step number 5.

   Make a list of your wife's negatives. Be honest *and* definite. Don't gloss over any part of the picture. Remember it's the *real* woman you are called to live with. Each of us married an ideal, but we are living with reality! A part of that reality is the negatives in your wife that are inconsistent with the ideal. Whether these qualities *should* be there or not is beside the point. The fact is they *are* there, and that's what you are called to live with.

   Don't get sidetracked by thinking: "But my wife is an earnest Christian. How *can* she act like that?"

   *Our inability to be objective and realistic about the negatives in our wives is one of the major hinderances to building a genuine love relationship to them.*

7. Make a similar list for each of your children.

8. Ask yourself some honest questions about these negatives.

   a. How many of them really *need* to change?

      Are you sure you are seeing each negative objectively? How important is it in the overall picture? Are you making a mountain out of a mole-hill?

      It bothered me that Jill could be so casual about some things that I felt were very important. But one day I began to see I had magnified their importance out of all proportion to reality. When I looked at those same things in relation to the overall picture of our family and life-work, they lost much of their importance. You who are perfectionists need to learn

107

that God is at peace with much that's imperfect. That was a hard lesson for me to learn. But as I did I found it *was possible* for me to be happy and at peace with others *while* they were imperfect, even my wife! After all, I'm far from perfect myself!

b. How much have you seriously prayed about the items on your list?

Remember, if they are really wrong, since God loves the person, He must want them changed too.

c. Along with praying, do you *expect* God to change them?

We often pray with a wistful hope, but with an inner doubt that God will actually *do something* about our situation. If you can't really trust Him, tell Him so, otherwise you'll probably resort to nagging, pushing, or just plain sulking. It's tough to discover that perhaps the *real* problem is your unbelief, not your wife!

d. Would it help if your attitude was different?

An encouraging, positive and helpful attitude can do wonders. A negative, nagging or critical attitude is devastating.

Most men resist being "pushed" by their wives. Don't you find your spirit rebelling if she starts nagging you?

Your wife is no different. Something in her resists pushing, scolding or a critical spirit. Try to understand, encourage and help her. This builds confidence, appreciation and trust in her which will stimulate responsiveness.

Years ago Jill found spring cleaning of our big old house a horrible mountain-like burden. It didn't seem big to me. I grew up on the farm where work was a challenge, so I would become impatient and pushy about the annual spring struggle.

God began to deal with me about my attitude. I saw how lacking in understanding I was. Looking at work only through my own experience, I failed completely to see the issue from Jill's point of view.

One day as Jill was expressing her dread of facing spring housecleaning, I found myself responding in a totally new way.

"Honey," I said, "Why don't you divide the whole job into small parts. Stop looking at the whole house, but just one room at a time. Decide on how much time you will allot to one room and when you've finished that room consider it a job completed. Then take the next room and approach it the same way. Before you know it the whole project will be completed."

"Darling," Jill exclaimed, "I never thought about it that way. Thank you for your suggestion. Dreading the job wears me out more than the actual work!"

I'm grateful for God's faithfulness to show me how negative I'd been, and for pointing out a better way.

It could help to jot down instances you can recall where a positive and helpful attitude has brought a change in others. Maybe you've seen it at work, in church, in your home or neighborhood. Recalling such examples will encourage you to look for more ways where you can apply this principle in your own home.

9. Make ditches for love.

Love is like a stream. It needs channels through which to flow. But we have to make the channels!

a. Words:

It helps to say "I love you," but there are other words that are equally important; like words of appreciation, expressions of encouragement and words of honesty spoken lovingly.

An African Christian told me that the two hardest words the Christians in his area had had to learn were the two little words, "I'm sorry."

When did you last ask your wife to forgive you? Or tell her "thank you" for some little thing she did? Or say "please" when you requested some small favor?

As you say loving words, and speak in a loving way, love itself will begin to flow. Stop a minute and think. What can you say to her today by way of appreciation or encouragement?

b. Actions:

There is power in a loving touch and in deeds done deliberately in love. Paul speaks of this in Romans 12:20, 21:

"If thine enemy hunger, feed him; if he thirst, give him to drink; for in so doing thou shalt heap coals of fire upon his head. Be not overcome of evil, but overcome evil with good."

Treat your enemy by loving him. Through feelings? No, through deeds or actions. Overwhelm him with kindness!

Try this principle at home. See how many ways you can discover for showing love through deeds. You did it when you were courting. What happened? Why not start again, not because you *feel* loving, but because you choose to show love deliberately. Stop a

110

minute *now* and think. What can you *do* for your wife *today* to communicate your love for her?

Many marriages would be saved if couples would be realistic enough to begin to cultivate love *deliberately*. Try holding hands. Walk arm in arm. Work at *showing* love, and you will be rewarded by *feeling* it.

10. Ask for love from God, and take it from Him by an attitude of faith.

    I've left this to the last because it's the most important.

    Ultimately the kind of love we are talking about *must come from God*. Only His love is adequate for the realities of human selfishness and the fallen world in which we live. But this love has already been made available to us:

    > ". . . the love of God hath been shed abroad in our hearts through the Holy Spirit which was given unto us."                                   Romans 5:5

    Having asked for this love, do you sit down in passive resignation until you get waves of loving feelings for your wife and children? No!

    Ask, take by faith, and thank God for the love *He has now given*, even without feelings. Then do *all you do* in an attitude of love, and in the *confidence* that the love really *is* there, not in the degree that you feel it, but because God is faithful. He has promised you love. You have asked for love and now you can trust Him for it *as you act it*.

    \*   \*   \*   \*   \*

*Love is a very tender plant. It needs lots of cultivating.*

111

# 11

## Consideration—Is It Old Fashioned?

"Each counting the other person better than himself."

Paul

"Bruce did you get the bike out of the garage for Linda?"

"No, but I will," answered Bruce.

Bruce was visiting his fiancée in her parent's home. They were the "gentleman — lady" type, reflecting the culture, values and way of life of the "good family" tradition of an earlier generation. Linda's father was the "old school gentleman" in every sense of the word. Thoroughly Christian, with sterling character, he treated his wife with that courtesy, respect and gracious consideration which seems to be found more in storybooks than in real life.

To be in Linda's home was a totally new experience

for Bruce. It was like living in a different world. Family members were continually expressing consideration for one another. Thoughtfulness and unselfishness seemed to be a way of life. The peace and harmony in that home were so different from the jangle, confusion and lack of consideration for others that characterized the home in which Bruce had grown up.

While the experience was new to Bruce, and at times quite unsettling to him, he found that he liked it immensely. People in Linda's home just expected others to be considerate, and they in turn expected to express consideration. While Bruce felt quite threatened at times by his lack of familiarity with the "ground rules" in his new setting, he was willing to learn.

So, when his father-in-law-to-be asked that question about the bike, Bruce got the message. It hadn't dawned on him to get the bike out of the garage for Linda. After all the garage door was wide open and the bicycle leaned against the wall just inside. Linda was perfectly able-bodied and quite capable of wheeling it out those few feet before riding to town.

The incident did something for Bruce. He began to watch his attitude and actions around Linda's home and compare them with what he saw demonstrated in countless little ways by her family. Linda's mother was every inch a lady, and yet she had that wonderful ability to put people at ease. She seemed to sense intuitively what their needs were and know how to meet them. She adored her husband whose leadership she obviously respected and delighted to follow. Linda's father was devoted to her mother, for whom he would do anything consistent with appropriateness and his abilities to make her happy. To

113

Bruce these two older people, into whose family circle he was soon to be joined, were a living expression of that directive in the New Testament:

> "Make full my joy, that you be of the same mind, having the same love, being of one accord, of one mind; doing nothing through faction or through vainglory, but in lowliness of mind each counting other better than himself; not looking each of you to his own things, but each of you also to the things of others."
>                                                    Phil. 2:2–4

Although Bruce knew these verses well, this was the first time he had seen them lived within the intimacy of a family circle.

*   *   *   *   *

Consideration of others is just another way of expressing the old-fashioned idea of courtesy.

Courtesy is consideration in action.

Courtesy is the opposite of selfishness.

Courtesy is an essential ingredient of true love. It's expression flows out of the practice of putting one's self in another person's place, and then applying in each situation those beautiful words of Jesus Christ:

> "All things therefore whatsoever you would that men should do unto you, even so do you also unto them. . ."
>                                                Matthew 7:12

There is a beauty, richness and deep satisfaction that is inherent in wholesome human relationships. But all too often these finer dimensions in family life seem to be missing. The idea of a man being a "Christian gentleman" seems to belong more to the past than to the present.

We don't deliberately plan it that way. Few husbands

114

*mean* to be inconsiderate, thoughtless or unkind. But all too often we are, and the results are nearly as devastating as though we meant to be both thoughtless *and* unkind.

What are some of the causes that contribute to the increasing scarcity of true consideration?

## SELF-CENTEREDNESS

We seldom think of self-centeredness as sin. We accept Christ in order to escape hell and get to heaven. We are urged to be all-out committed Christians in order to gain heavenly rewards, become fulfilled as persons, or to repay in some degree a debt of love we owe Jesus Christ. But in comparatively few cases are we brought face to face with the fact that self-centeredness is just another form of old-fashioned sin. Writers of a past age called it the sin of inordinate self-love. It is one expression of basic spiritual immaturity.

A self-centered man is more concerned with what *he* wants, how *he* feels and what *he* gets, than he is by how his wife feels, what she wants or what she gets. Such a man is often insensitive in his attitudes toward his family. He is wrapped up in his own interests, plans, and projects. He doesn't seem to notice when he inconveniences others or hurts them.

For some men this type of immaturity is expressed in moods or periods of depression and stony silence. He may stay late at the office, hibernate behind the newspaper or T.V., and when forced to be with his family at meal-time or in the car he will remain stolid and uncommunicative.*

* For a helpful discussion of moods see LeHaye, *How To Win Over Depression*, Zondervan, Grand Rapids, Michigan.

There is no simple or easy cure for self-centeredness, especially since it is so common and is often regarded as perfectly legitimate. With the major emphasis on *getting* in life rather than *giving,* the self-centered man *who wants to change* will find the going tough and slow. Change is made more difficult because the various expressions of self-centeredness become life-patterns which grow more deeply rooted the older we get.

Conviction by the Holy Spirit of the sinfulness of self-centeredness is basic to any significant change. But conviction from God often follows cooperative effort on our part. There are some steps any man can take RIGHT NOW!

1. Take a few minutes each day for one week to evaluate your motives in family relationships. Are your personal activities motivated by self-interest or by a desire to benefit your wife and children?

2. List several specific instances in a typical day that indicate you really want to be less self-centered.

   Nate began to realize he expected to be waited on at meal time. It dawned on him that he would habitually ask Marge to get a forgotten spoon or some article that was missing at the table. It hadn't occurred to him that she too was tired, and that he was quite capable of getting up quietly and without a negative comment get the missing item himself.

   As Nate began to be more considerate of Marge in this one little area he began to be alert to his self-centeredness in many other ways. This led to a growing conviction that much of his life had been lived purely for himself. As the sinfulness of his past ways dawned upon his mind, Nate was driven to God for forgiveness and

116

cleansing. A new spirit of graciousness and consideration is now evident in Nate's family life.

We tend to think of conviction by the Holy Spirit as a sudden and vivid awareness of our sinfulness, usually accompanied by strong emotions of guilt and a crisis experience of repentance and God-given forgiveness. Those who have this idea of conviction often spend months or years waiting passively for God to bring such an experience to them.

Instead of this, conviction is more often like a tiny ray of light in your mind that awakens your conscience to a seemingly insignificant "wrong" in your behaviour. Obedient response to this light brings more light. Then, before you are aware of it, major changes are taking place in your life style!

Don't "wait for conviction" as something that must happen before you change. Begin acting on what you see now. As you obey in little things, more light will follow.

> "Light obeyed increases light.
> Light rejected bringeth night."

"The path of the righteous is as the dawning light that shineth more and more unto the perfect day."     Proverbs 4:18

## BUSYNESS

We had lived abroad and in several countries for a few years. It was Sunday morning when the little Irish freighter on which we were returning to America came into radio range of the U.S. eastern seaboard. The ship's radio was tuned to a New York station, and suddenly we found ourselves listening to a typical American church service. Jill and I looked startled! The hymns were sung at such a fast tempo! Everything had a disturbing rush about it. Was this *our* country? Had *we* sung in that light and frightfully rapid beat? Rush! Movement! Activity! Hurry! Bustle! This seems to be characteristic of America — and increasingly of the great metropolitan centers of the world. Life at a quiet pace is a rarity today. And the faster the jets fly the tighter the traveling man packs his schedule.

Consideration takes time — and thought. It is difficult to remember the little niceties when the pressure of living has ensnared us in its vortex. How often is your family caught up in life's mad whirl? Business — work — school — community activities — church — club — a seemingly endless number of involvements clamor for our attention and time.

The relaxed evening over dinner in the dining room is replaced by a hurried meal in the breakfast nook. Dad is rushing to get to a board meeting. Kristin is fidgety about her date with Steve. Junior bolts his food so he can get to ball practice. Mother wonders how she can possibly clear up before the ladies arrive for this month's discussion on ways to improve family relationships!

While the rat-race of today's life-style contributes in many ways to the overall breakdown of the home, perhaps in no way are its effects more unrecognized than in the subtle erosion of consideration. When people stop being considerate *they start taking each other for granted.* In an unrealized way they stop being real people and become more like part of the furniture or the fixtures around the house.

When we take people for granted we start making

demands of them that may be unreasonable. Hurts and resentments result. Communication breaks down. Irritations grow. Almost without realizing it the fragrance and beauty of family living disappear. And yet, nobody has done anything *really* wrong! We were all just too busy.

Stop your world and step off. Take a deep breath. Relax five minutes. Now take a good honest look at yourself and your family. Are you more considerate of your secretary than you are of your wife? Can you dash off to work with hardly a pleasant goodbye to Sandra, irked because the eggs were burned, then greet the gals at the office with the sweet niceties of the gracious gentleman?

How can you beat the battle of busyness? Take a leaf from successful management:

1. Set aside time for a realistic evaluation of your family situation as it is.
2. List all the activities in which you and your family are involved. What are the time and frequency factors of these activities?
3. Set aside an evening for a family conference on this general subject.
4. Map out your "activity profile" on a calendar so you can see where you are doubled up or where you may have free time of which you were unaware.
5. List your priorities and evaluate them.
6. Discuss as a family some practical steps for reducing the feeling of hurry and pressure in your home.
7. Place high on your priority list having time to be together as a family and/or as a couple.
8. Plan "family times" and put them into your date book.

   Larry was a busy corporate executive whose responsibilities involved frequent trips away from home. Increasingly the pressures of a growing family, activities at church and in the community, and the demands of his job brought a subtle depersonalization of family relationships. Brought up short by an almost tragic crisis at home, Larry stopped long enough to re-evaluate. He noticed that Saturday mornings were usually free and that he was seldom away on weekends. He felt that one helpful step toward better relationships at home would be for Heather and him to have some regular uninterrupted time together, away from their children and away from the phone.

Since the children were old enough to be left alone for a few hours, Larry and Heather agreed to go out for breakfast on Saturday mornings. This gave them time to be together, to think and to plan. These times of unhurried sharing of their thoughts and feelings have done much to bring about a new awareness of each other. Tensions have been reduced in the family and a wholesomely different spirit pervades their home.

## MATERIALISM

We are molded by our values! Personality, character and behavior patterns are affected by those things which are most important to us. Charles Dickens, in *A Christmas Carol,* has drawn in old Scrooge the classic illustration of this unalterable principle. Scrooge was wedded to his gold, and like the hard and lifeless metal to which he gave himself, he became a cold, heartless, impersonal thing.

None of us plans to be a Scrooge. Nor did he. It happens so gradually. Bit by bit we give ourselves to that which we consider important and we become shaped accordingly.

At no time in history have the cold, hard, and lifeless material "things" in life loomed so important as they do today to the average American. Credit card buying, modern advertising techniques, and our general affluence work together to increase our built-in proneness to impulse purchasing. Built-in obsolescence, rapid and drastic fashion changes, and high pressure sales tactics add to our impulsive desires the conviction that we can't get along without that new "thing" — be it carpet, boat, new clothes or microwave oven.

In addition to the goal of accumulation of things is the deeper commitment to *material success* as a legitimate and desirable reason for being. America is unique in that material attainment is at least a possibility for nearly any person with average intelligence, normal health, and the willingness to pay the price of hard work, ingenuity and dedication.

But in the process of achieving the highest standard of living on earth (materially speaking), we have paid a fearful price in terms of broken hearts, shattered homes and a fragmented society. Married to material possessions, we have become, like the "things" we have chosen, insensitive to people. The great American dream contains the seeds of its own decay. We hewed our civilization out of a wilderness. Men climbed from rags to riches, and from humble cottages to the White House. But in pursuing our goals we have lost our heart.

Some friends were having dinner in the home of a Christian who had just been promoted to a high position in a large corporation. He was American success personified. He began with nothing, and now had everything. In the midst of the conversation his wife, an earnest Christian, spoke up. Her words were quiet but penetrating,

"Don't forget, dear, what success has cost the family!"

\* \* \* \* \*

A friend asked to meet me for lunch. As he opened his heart it was just one more demonstration of the price men pay for material success. He had been offered an enviable promotion in his corporation. As Al and his wife prayed about the offer, it became increasingly clear that for them the promotion would prove detrimental to their family life as well as to their spiritual well-being. He declined to accept, and ultimately was given the option of resigning or being fired.

"There is no place on the corporate team for a man who refuses to move up," Al was told.

Sticking to the decision Al and his wife made, he resigned. Upon receiving the resignation, Al's top boss, who had previously threatened him, called him into his private office. With tears running down his face he said:

"Al, you have had the guts to do what years ago I should have done but didn't have the courage to do. I have position, power and money, but I've lost my soul, my family and my God. I envy and admire you."

The very heart of the home is consideration for its members. The day to day expression of your consideration for your family will be determined by the practical value you attach to the many material things which are so much a part of life as we know it today.

What can you do about this?

1. Ask some honest questions:

    a. Are you more committed to your work than you are to the total well-being of your family?

b. What is your *real* purpose for living?

c. Would you be content with a less demanding job with a smaller income, if by this you could have a more satisfying family life?

d. Do you feel driven by your work?

e. Are you uptight over financial pressures created by unwise and perhaps unnecessary buying?

f. Have you subconsciously substituted providing a nice home and all that goes with it for the day to day development of wholesome, happy people-relationships in your family?

2. Evaluate your personal and family life-style. Is it centered in things or in people? Are you so committed to obtaining and maintaining things that there is little time or heart for the individuals in your family?

A Christian couple had a Christmas party for a large group of friends. Their home was immaculate, tastefully furnished, and beautifully decorated for the season and the occasion. As I commended the host for their beautiful home and thanked him for the delightful evening, he quietly replied, "Yes, this evening cost us two weeks of migraines."

There is a beautiful story in Luke 10:38–42. Jesus was invited to the home of two sisters, Martha and Mary. Martha planned a big dinner and became very involved in all that it takes to put one on. Mary, instead of helping her sister, spent the time visiting with Jesus. In exasperation Martha asked her guest to please tell Mary to go into the kitchen and help her. After all, wasn't she trying to give an extra nice dinner? As the story puts it, "Martha was cumbered (distracted) about much serving." Jesus' reply to Martha is most interesting: "Martha, Martha, you are anxious and troubled about many things. . ." And He didn't ask Mary to go to her sister's aid!

Can you imagine the conflict that probably raged in Martha's heart? But the root of her problem was *over*-concern about "things" in life, not the seeming unfairness of her sister leaving her all the work.

It is the being *burdened* about many things, that so subtly kills the graciousness of consideration in a family.

3. Discuss with your family the subject of materialism as it affects your family relationships. Come up with practical suggestions for guarding against being corrupted by too great an attachment to things and adding more.

4. Face honestly the fact, clearly stated in the Bible, that all we are and have is really God's and is only loaned to us as a sacred trust. What a tragedy if the gifts on loan to us become the cause of our own corruption. To pursue this further look at I Chronicles 29:11–17; Psalm 24:1; Matthew 25:14–30; Ephesians 4:28; Luke 12:13–21.

5. Think of ways you could use your possessions for the blessing of others. In this way you will become a channel for good, and God's gifts to you will not harm you. A lake with no outlet becomes stagnant and foul. The same lake used as a source for irrigation becomes a reservoir of life. Study Luke 3:11; Matthew 25:31–46; Acts 10:1–4; Proverbs 11:24–26; II Corinthians 9:6–11.

There are many other causes contributing to the lack of true consideration in our homes, but most of them stem from the three basic causes mentioned above. Be aware that life will get more hectic, not less. Our society is moving steadily toward greater depersonalization, less need for people around us, greater mechanization, increasing living and job transcience. There is an accelerated disappearance of the ideals of chivalry, with the marked erasure of the finer distinctions between men and women. You and I will have to live in the world as it is, regardless of what we would like it to be. It is important, therefore, that we take positive steps to develop genuine consideration in our family relationships.

Here are several suggestions:

1. Identify the areas where your consideration of your wife and children needs to be improved. Look at your daily habits. In what ways do you seek to conform your habits to the convenience of others?

    a. List some things you do which indicate you are sensitive to the needs of your wife and children.

    b. Note three instances this week showing you are alert to opportunities to help them or make life easier or more enjoyable for them.

    c. How do *they* know that you are interested in the things that concern them, or that they are interested in?

    d. What indicates that you understand and appreciate their sense of values?

    e. Make a list of their hopes, fears, and aspirations.

2. Check your speech and communication patterns. Recall the past week.

    a. How many times have you monopolized the conversation?

    b. How often have you clammed up in rude silence?

    c. In how many conversations did you participate freely even though the subject didn't particularly interest you?

    d. How did you disagree? Can you present differing views without having to prove your point or make others feel threatened or belittled?

125

    e. Is your language courteous, clean and gracious? What is your tone of voice like?

    f. Do you speak at the age-level and emotional response of each member?

3. List areas you want to improve

Now look honestly and objectively at the list. Take only one or two of those areas and write down some practical steps that you can take to realize improvement. It might help to talk these over with your wife or possibly have a family conference on the subject — depending on the nature of the issues and the ages of your children.

> Burt realized he had a number of routine habits that were irritating to Nancy. Earlier in their marriage she had really nagged him about them, but finally had given up, since the more she had nagged, the more determined he had become not to be pushed around. Anyway, wasn't a man's home his castle? And why couldn't he do as he pleased in it?

> As a boy, Burt had never been made to pick up after himself. His mother had always hung up his clothes, made his bed, and cleaned his room. He now began to see how totally thoughtless he was in so many little areas of life.

> When Burt started to make a list of his habits that revealed lack of consideration, it surprised him how active his mind became. He began to see all kinds of ways in which he lived in a self-centered way. He would leave his clothes around for Nancy to pick up. She had to put his shaving gear away each morning. Instead of rinsing the sink after brushing his teeth, he would leave it. The tooth-paste rinsed from his mouth would dry in the sink, and Nancy would have to clean it before she could wash. Burt even thought of such a simple thing as putting the toilet seat down, so Nancy wouldn't have to.

But you don't need Burt's background to develop Burt's habits.

Dave saw marriage as his opportunity to throw off the rigid rules of courtesy and tidiness that his mother had imposed on him as a child.

Mike on the other hand grew up like a weed, as did his brothers and sisters. Their home had been a heap, so he had never been trained in any way.

## THE IMPORTANT THING IS *NOT* YOUR BACK-GROUND!!!

*The important thing is to identify an area where you need to improve, list some practical steps for improvement and get busy implementing those steps.* Habits aren't usually changed overnight. It took time for habits to be formed, and they are changed by developing a different set of habits. This takes time, a good attitude and — persistence!

In Burt's case he saw his self-centeredness so clearly that he apologized to Nancy and asked her to help him by reminding him when he reverted to the old way. Some of his expressions of inconsideration were so funny when isolated from the larger pattern that Burt and Nancy found themselves making a game out of it all. This gave the whole matter a happy light touch, minimizing the seriousness of it and taking a lot of the sting and humiliation away.

It's important that you see some actual improvement in one area before you make great plans in other areas. For some of us the easiest thing of all is to get some lists of needed changes down on paper.

We may be good at making plans for change.

*But what is needed in the end is change.*

127

If you can effect change that is observable in one area, you will be encouraged to move to other areas and to take other steps toward improvement.

DON'T PUT OFF MAKING A START. Every journey begins by taking the first step.

Lay down some ground rules, first for yourself, and then for your children. Many children never say "please" or "thank you" around the home or at the table because they haven't been trained, or, what is worse, they have never heard their father speak courteously at home. So establish some guidelines for expressing consideration like:

— Say "Please" when you ask for things.
— Say "Thank you" when you receive from others.
— Treat each other in the home courteously.
— Respect the right of privacy for each individual.
— Help each other learn to be helpful.
— Respect the rights of ownership, even with the smaller children, while at the same time learning to share your things.

Remember:

The underlying reason for inconsideration is self-centeredness. If you love your wife and children, you will work at being considerate of them.

*True love and self-centeredness cannot co-exist.*

# 12

# Remember—
# You're the Father of Her Children

The frightening changes and breath-taking swiftness of change have left older parents reeling and younger ones almost paralyzed with fear.

One common reaction to the disintegration of family is for us as fathers to bury ourselves more deeply in our work or to escape the problem by blaming the times.

However we may do it, hiding our heads in the sand won't change the facts of life or solve the problems that are suddenly confronting us.

The fact is, God has laid at the father's door the major responsibility for the development, discipline and training of his children.

". . . fathers, provoke not your children to wrath; but nurture them in the chastening and admonition of the Lord."

Ephesians 6:4

"For I have known him, to the end that he may command his children and his household after him that they may keep the way of the Lord, to do righteousness and justice; to the end that the Lord may bring upon Abraham that which he hath spoken of him?"                    Genesis 18:19

"For I have told him that I will judge his house forever, for the iniquity which he knew, because his sons did bring a curse upon themselves, and he restrained them not."
                                        I Samuel 3:13

The bishop must be "one that ruleth well his own house, having his children in subjection with all gravity."
                                        I Timothy 3:4

A large number of children and young people, reared in seemingly good Christian homes, have pretty well tuned out their parents. They seem to have decided that they'll look for their own answers and forget their elders who, they are sure, have been inadequate guides, invalid counselors and poor examples.

Regardless of the pros and cons of the shift in attitudes toward parents by our youth, you still have to accept the simple fact that you are the father of your children.

Whether you have succeeded, failed, or merely gotten along in your role is in one sense rather academic. Whatever your rating up or down the parental success scale, you must begin where you are now.

## WHOSE ARE THEY?

Some things in life have a finality about them. If you run over a man and kill him, the fact of his death is a rather final affair. Nothing you do will change it. The

130

sorrow, heartache, guilt, suffering and a thousand other implications won't change the stark reality that the man you ran down is no longer living.

In a similar way conception, pregnancy and birth have a finality about them. Whether a child was wanted or unwanted; whether you are able to cope with parenthood or not, are beside the point. Conception is the initiation of life. Even if you were not involved (as in the case of an adopted child) *you are the father!* And being the father means you have responsibilities. Your first responsibility is to recognize and accept a deeper reality: GOD IS THE AUTHOR AND GIVER OF LIFE!

> "For thou didst form my inward parts: thou didst cover me in my mother's womb." Psalm 139:13

> "Lo, children are a heritage of the Lord; and the fruit of the womb is his reward," Psalm 127:3

> "He maketh the barren woman to keep house, and to be a joyful mother of children." Psalm 113:8,9

> "And Isaac entreated the Lord for his wife, because she was barren: and the Lord was entreated of him, and Rebekah his wife conceived." Genesis 25:21

The child or children you beget or adopt are God's gifts to you and their mother. As gifts from Him they are to be:

— Accepted at conception.
— Cared for during pregnancy.
— Welcomed gladly at birth.
— Nurtured, trained and developed during their formative years.

It's one thing to accept children in theory or ideally. It's quite another to accept them in reality and within the context of difficult, pressured and demanding life-cir-cumstances. Each new child automatically ties its parents to a long-range responsibility. The only way to be sure you'll follow through on that responsibility is to lay the foundation of *right attitudes* even before your children are conceived.

If your family is already started or nearly grown, you need to be sure your attitudes about parenthood are wholesome and right.

Take time to settle with God and your own heart that each child *is* God's love-gift, whether planned for or not, and whether wanted by you and/or your wife or not.

Gifts are valued in a large degree by who did the giv-ing. If you have settled in your heart that the little bundle of life now developing in your wife is a love-gift from God, you will have a hard time being negative toward it in later months or years.

Just as you are living, not with the ideal you married, but with a real person who has both positives *and* nega-tives, so there are both positives and negatives in your children. Many parents want children in an abstract, ideal sort of way. Often these same parents find it difficult to accept their children as they really turn out to be — especially those who are unusually difficult or trouble-some. This may be particularly true if one or the other parents resented the child being conceived in the first place.

Stop reading for a minute. Either mentally or on paper jot down the names of your children. Under each name note everything you don't like about that child. If your dislike is strong enough to call it resentment, put a star in front of that trait.

Timmy:

| poor grades |
| * uncooperative at home |
| goofs off |
| always running around |
| doesn't take initiative |
| * sloppy |

Beth:

| moody |
| talks back to her mother |
| * fights with Timmy |
| * does her work around home with a bad spirit |

Now try switching roles. Put yourself in their place and imagine yourself as the child with a father like you. What do you believe you'd want from a dad if you were in their shoes.

Make a list of them, like —

— interested *in me*
— makes time for me
— talks and listens
— understands my problems
— loves me even when I goof off
— explains the rules
— doesn't keep nagging

Now ask some questions:

Is what you think they'd want from you reasonable?

Could you, as their dad, provide it?

What would have to change if you were to try?

Take the time to talk this over with each child. If you

133

can't provide what you have reason to believe he wants, explain to him why. If you expect to start, tell him so — but only if you really plan to follow through. But be sure to share with him the fact that it will take time for you to change, and at times you may fail. Tell him you'll need his patience and help to fulfill your role as a father adequately.


## DELEGATION

Whole-hearted acceptance of each child must be accompanied by genuine, willing acceptance of your role and responsibility as father. This goes far beyond being a good provider.

> "Honestly, I've slaved all my married life to give my son a decent upbringing, and now he's flipped."

\* \* \* \* \*

> "What do you mean, be a good father? Compared to what I had as a kid, my crew has lived on easy street. When I got married I determined I'd never see my kids go without like I did as a boy. And I've reached that goal. They've had it good, at least in my way of thinking. But do they appreciate all I've done? It sure doesn't look like it to me. And now you suggest I haven't been a good father! You've gotta be kidding."

\* \* \* \* \*

> "Look, my job is to see that my family is cared for, and that's what I've been doing. We've had decent food to eat, the house is nearly paid for, and there's enough in prospect for the kids to go to college. I've even managed to lay up a bit of a nest egg just in case we get some rainy days down the road.

"Of course it's taken a lot of nose-to-the-grindstone living. I haven't been able to spare time for foolishness with the kids. My boys and I don't talk much. Working two jobs plus overtime doesn't give much time for non-essential extras like church and what all the experts call "family times". But I've done a good job.

"My idea of being the right kind of father is to make sure the wolf doesn't get too near the door. As far as running the home and managing the kids are concerned, well, that's the wife's job. Sometimes she complains a bit about me not being home enough, or for not taking time when I am home to play and goof around with our boys. But I notice they don't mind riding in that new car I'm having to make payments on.

"A fellow needs to delegate. That's how I've managed. A guy can't do everything. Keeping bread on the table and a little for extras now and then is a big order in my opinion. And I'm glad I've got a smart gal like Brenda who really runs a tight ship at home so I don't have to worry. Her department is to manage the family. My job is to provide what it takes to keep it running."

\* \* \* \* \*

What is the major mistake that's common to each of these typical stories of American family life?

A large percentage of American fathers have assumed wrongly that being good providers for the family's physical needs discharges them from other major responsibilities. We've done a neat cop-out on the *real issue* of fatherhood!

In the chapter on leadership we discussed the problem of the American husband opting for being a good provider in exchange for fulfilling his role as leader in his home. The application in that section was primarily to his wife, for every woman down underneath wants the security of her husband's leadership of love.

The failure to accept our full responsibility as fathers is only an extension of our failure to fulfill our role as leaders. And we cover it all by a neat rationalization that our major job is to be adequate providers while superficially delegating the management of the children to their mother.

Do you realize that while you may delegate responsibility, you *cannot delegate accountability?* God holds you and me ultimately accountable for the rearing of our children.

Eli, the high priest, was charged by God with delinquency in the managing of his two wayward sons.

> "And the Lord said to Samuel, Behold I will do a thing in Israel, at which both the ears of every one that heareth it shall tingle. In that day I will perform against Eli all that I have spoken concerning his house, from the beginning even unto the end. For I have told him that I will judge his house for ever, for the iniquity which he knew, because his sons did bring a curse upon themselves, and he restrained them not. And therefore I have sworn unto the house of Eli, that the iniquity of Eli's house shall not be expiated with sacrifice nor offering for ever." I Samuel 3:11–14

The Bible states that it was David who spoiled his son Adonijah prior to the young man's attempt to usurp the throne which was to be given to Solomon.

> "Then Adonijah the son of Haggith exalted himself, saying, I will be king: and he prepared him chariots and horsemen, and fifty men to run before him. And his father had not displeased him at any time in saying, why hast thou done

so? and he was also a very goodly man; and he was born
after Absalom," I Kings 1:5,6

Eli and David were busy men with heavy responsibilities outside the home. Nevertheless the demands of their careers did not excuse them from being accountable to God for managing their children.

Would it help for you to re-think your goals and your priorities? Have you faced the fact that it's much easier, less threatening and less demanding to be buried in the job than to provide over-all leadership for a growing family? Often the rewards of the job are more immediate, tangible, and exciting than what you get at home. After all, you don't get a raise in pay or a promotion to status and power by being a competent father.

You may need to rethink your job responsibilities if you accept what is involved in being an adequate dad. Talk your situation over with your wife. Pray much about it and then expect God to guide you clearly.

If in your heart you've really accepted the fact that you are accountable to God for your children, there can be a great deal of flexibility in working out the mechanics.

There's nothing wrong with *genuine* delegation—as long as you retain the accountability. Real delegation isn't a haphazard affair. You have to work at it, with constant open communication between the people concerned.

Your role as father includes your responsibility as provider. The two need not be in conflict, nor does God intend that the roles should clash. If you are willing to work them out, God will give you and your family the needed wisdom. Be sure your heart is truly willing, and that you are really committed to your family.

137

# 13

## Example—Good or Bad?

**Junior Will Try to Walk in Dad's Shoes**

A teenage boy walked out of his home one day with the exclamation, "If that's religion, I've had it!"

His dad's intentions were good and his profession sincere, but his example was totally inconsistent with what he professed to believe.

The family was faithful and active in their church.

Family devotions were regular.

But the boy's father had never learned to control his temper or let go his worrying. The family took the brunt of the father's worried brooding and the outbursts of his uncontrolled temper.

Involved in fatherhood is the awesome responsibility of providing for our children a climate conducive to growth. There needs to be a realistic example of those values, behavior patterns, and interpersonal relationships which Scripture, reason and conscience affirm to be desirable. It is not enough for you to tell your children how you want them to act, or even to enforce your teaching by a variety of excellent family rules.

*They must see dad demonstrate* in his own life what he teaches.

"Do as I say but not as I do" may serve as an easy attitude to get dad off the hook, but it's both wrong and destructive to have a double standard in the home. Children learn most of what they really know through observation, and they imitate what they see in their parents. They will tend to do what *you do* rather than what you say.

Most of us are quite careful about *what we believe* about life, but all too frequently are casual about *how we live it.*

One day I began to realize how careful I was to insist on the children being frugal in their use of money, while I found myself spending quite easily for a cup of coffee or other incidentals whenever I felt like it.

We had a rule about food: "You don't have to like it; you just have to eat it." But I could weasel out of the rule by clueing my wife ahead of time not to prepare dishes I didn't like!

The Holy Spirit began to check me in many "little" areas where I, as dad, was frightfully inconsistent.

Like —

— I was very glad my wife stayed positive and encouraged me when I made mistakes or failed. But it seemed I was miserably critical when the children didn't measure up to my expectations.

— It was easy for me to insist the children learn self-discipline, but how slow I was to practice it for myself.

139

An effective way to remain up-to-date on your being an example is periodically to have a family conference. Include everyone and as a group agree on a number of important points:

1. That all of you — including dad — need God's continual motivation and enablement to live as you should.
2. For this reason you will pray regularly for each other, especially that God will undertake for specific needs, weaknesses and sins.
3. That you will maintain a policy of openness and loving honesty with each other, sharing with each other those areas where each of you needs specific prayer.
4. That you will discuss as a family your standards and how well you are living up to them.

If you as a parent will be honest, open and free in sharing with the children your need for God's grace and their help in being the person and parent you should be, it's amazing how honest and helpful the children will be toward you. Even small children have a keen sense of justice. They will respond with openness and honesty when treated fairly by elders.

Part of being fair is to admit when you are wrong and to ask for forgiveness. This is a very important part of being an example to your children.

Your example must demonstrate what you hold to be right and appropriate in three areas:

— Values

— Behavior patterns (life-style)

— Interpersonal relationships

140

## DEMONSTRATION OF RIGHT VALUES

To profess a relationship to Jesus Christ, Lord of an eternal kingdom, and to live for the perishing tangibles of this world is the height of inconsistency. At the same time, living for the eternal world does not release us from earthly obligations and involvements.

How can you train your child to live in a world of "things" (money, land, houses, time, jobs, possessions), carry responsibility in this world, have possessions, earn and save money, and yet live for an eternal world whose values are on an entirely different plane and of a different nature?

The most effective and the simplest way is for you to demonstrate your teaching by your life. This means you have to make sure that you really have given God the practical ownership of all you are and have. Your body, mind, time, family, job, money, house, and even hobbies and vacations are temporals — *loaned to you by God*. They are a sacred trust from God, to be used for God, and one day will be accounted for to God. With you setting the example, money should become important to your children, but in a different way than it is to the average person. As they observe your attitude toward it and your use of it, they will understand what it means to earn it, hold it and then use it as a sacred trust. The same will be true of the other tangibles in life, such as time, opportunity, the human body, clothes, cars, and the whole category of "things".

There are other values which are eternal in nature but which must be embraced and developed in this life.

141

These too need to be demonstrated if they are to be seen and desired by our children.

What practical value do you place on integrity, truthfulness, purity, diligence, laughter, joyfulness, compassion, tenderness, bravery, loyalty to God — to country — to family and friends? These values relate to personal character and spiritual realities.

The choices you make daily reveal to your children the nature of your values. God says:

"A good name is rather to be chosen than great riches. . ."
Proverbs 22:1

It's one thing to teach your children the importance of having and keeping a good name. But it's far more effective to demonstrate what you mean by the daily choices you make. You may be careful about major choices, but it's the many little choices that reveal what you really are. You are unconsciously speaking to your children just as much in the seemingly unimportant decisions as in those larger crisis decisions of life. So, ask yourself, "What am I demonstrating in issues like: refraining from gossip, honesty, integrity, keeping speed limits, punctuality, etc." Life is lived, taught and learned, "line upon line, line upon line; here a little, there a little." Isaiah 28:10.

These daily insignificant choices determine what we will do in the moments of crisis or once-in-a-lifetime opportunities. *Our children must learn a way of life, not just the making of a crisis choice.*

What do your little choices reveal of your life-values? What kinds of choices do you make when the pressure is off and you are "free" — at home — on vacation — Sunday afternoon? *Ask yourself what you would learn about life values if you were your son watching you live day by day?*

We are not born with character already formed. We are born with personality, but character has to be developed. This development occurs as we make daily, often unconscious choices, and our choices follow what our heart's love. Sooner or later each of us does what we really want to do.


## DEMONSTRATING RIGHT BEHAVIOR PATTERNS

Probably at no time in modern history has there been such a frightening rate of change. The net result is that people are increasingly free to determine their own individual life-style, code of ethics, standards of conduct or overall behavior patterns. In the midst of such a maze of relative values our children will be developing patterns of behavior that are either right or wrong. The way you and I as dads live our lives will have a lot to do with the kinds of patterns our children develop.

You may never have thought about it specifically, but you do have a code of ethics, and you follow your own particular value system and life-style. To certain elements of your life pattern you have attached a degree of morality. In my boyhood home it was almost a sin to leave food on my plate, but manners at the table seemed relatively unimportant. We ran a small diary, bottled the milk and delivered it to residential customers. Dad was very particular that the milk house be kept spotless and neat, but the way we kept our rooms was ignored. It was very important that we children make good grades in school, but to have clothes in style was of no consequence.

The problem is that many of us are not helping our children form a solid base upon which to develop their patterns for living.

Some parents have insisted their children behave like a past generation. Others have abandoned all attempts to enforce any coherent pattern for living, leaving their children with no real guide-lines for making choices. In either case, the parent has really demonstrated his basic life values.

Take the question of hair styles, grooming and dress for our young people. A great deal of heat has been generated over this. Homes have been psychologically, if not physically fractured as a result of the conflict. The rigidity seen in many parents was amazing. How many took time to think through the whole issue honestly and unemotionally?

It came as a shock to me when I realized how rigid I was and how little time I had given to thinking the issue through for myself. By my attitude and example I was communicating loudly and clearly to my family that my life-style was right! To me there was *no other way*. What I failed to see at first was the importance of helping my children arrive at a solid basis of their own for making valid decisions.

Who said it is "right" to wear a tie to church, and "wrong" not to? Since when did it become "sinful" to have a beard? Why is a suit more "holy" than blue jeans? Did God ordain a specific style for men's hair?

For a time it was easy to be right in my rigid, conservative life-style, until I had to face youth's searching question, "But Dad, what's *wrong* with wearing blue jeans to church?"

With a jolt, I realized I had never thought many things through for myself, and consequently was unable to help my teens think through the deeper issues out of which spring a host of specific questions.

I was giving my children an example of *a* way of life, but I was not showing them *why* I chose that way of life! Nor was I helping them develop an understanding of those underlying issues that would guide them in developing their own life-style.

Related to this whole issue is the fundamental fact that there are constants as well as variables in life. Some things are clearly right or wrong. Others are not. Have you been able to help your children learn how to tell the difference between constants and variables and follow through with appropriate personal decisions?

What are some guidelines for determining what is right? How can we distinguish between the constants that never change and the variables that fluctuate from age to age, from one part of the country to another, and even from situation to situation?

The answer is not simplistic but there are four underlying principles upon which to build.

1. *What does the Bible say,* either by specific statement or general teaching? e.g. It states categorically that adultery (unfaithfulness in the marriage relationship) is sin.

   "Let marriage be had in honor among all, and let the bed be undefiled: for fornicators and adulterers God will judge."                    Hebrews 13:4

   It also teaches plainly that all relationships between the sexes must be morally pure. But it *does not* state whether it is right or wrong for an unengaged couple to hold hands or kiss on a date!

". . . Your body is a temple of the Holy Spirit which is in you, which you have from God? And you are not your own; for you were bought with a price: Glorify God therefore in your body."  I Corinthians 6:19, 20

"Know ye not that the unrighteous shall not inherit the Kingdom of God? Be not deceived: neither fornicators, nor idolaters, nor adulterers, nor effeminate, nor abusers of themselves with men, nor thieves, nor covetous, nor drunkards, nor revilers, nor extortioners, shall inherit the Kingdom of God."

I Corinthians 6:9, 10

The above is a list of activities which are specifically prohibited by God. The list includes covetousness. But the Bible does not tell us exactly where the line is found between working to earn our living (which we are commanded to do) and coveting (which is sin).

Our behavior must accord with both the specific commands and the general teaching of the Bible.

2. *God is holy.* His holiness is demonstrated by the life and character of Jesus Christ as well as being taught in the Bible.

"As children of obedience, not fashioning yourselves according to your former lusts in the time of your ignorance: but like as he who called you is holy, be ye yourselves also holy in all manner of living; because it is written, ye shall be holy; for I am holy."

I Peter 1:14–16

". . .Christ also suffered for you, leaving you an example, that ye should follow his steps; who did no sin, neither was guile found in his mouth; who, when he was reviled, reviled not again; when he suffered, threatened not; but committed himself to Him that judgeth righteously:"  I Peter 3:21–23

146

"I coveted no man's silver, or gold, or apparel. Ye yourselves know that these hands ministered to my own necessities, and to them that were with me. In all things I gave you an example, that so laboring ye ought to help the weak, and to remember the words of the Lord Jesus, that Himself said, It is more blessed to give than to receive." Acts 20:33–35

"Now we that are strong ought to bear the infirmities of the weak, and not to please ourselves . . . for Christ also pleased not Himself; but as it is written, the reproaches of them that reproached thee fell upon me." Romans 15:1–3

"Doing nothing through faction or through vainglory, but in lowliness of mind each counting other better than himself . . . Have this mind in you which was also in Christ Jesus. . ." Philippians 2:3–5

There must be harmony between our daily living and the character of our holy God.

3. *The great law of love,* called by James the "Royal Law": "Thou shalt love thy neighbor as thyself," which he says we shall do well if we fulfill. James 2:8

"Thou shalt love the Lord thy God with all thy heart, and with all thy soul, and with all thy mind." Matthew 22:37

"Owe no man anything, save to love one another: for he that loveth his neighbor hath fulfilled the law. For this, Thou shalt not commit adultery,
Thou shalt not kill,
Thou shalt not steal,
Thou shalt not covet . . . and if there be any other commandment, it is summed up in this word: Thou shalt love thy neighbor as thyself."

> "Love worketh no ill to his neighbor: love therefore is
> the fulfillment of the law."        Romans 13:8–10

Behavior must demonstrate this law of love which lies at
the heart of God and of His eternal Kingdom.

4. *Our behavior must bring glory to God* and promote the interests of His eternal kingdom. Besides this we will give an
   accounting to God for the way we have lived this life.

   > "Whether therefore ye eat, or drink, or whatsoever ye
   > do, do all to the glory of God."     I Corinthians 10:31

   > "And whatsoever ye do, in word or in deed, do all in
   > the name of the Lord Jesus, giving thanks to God the
   > Father through Him."        Colossians 3:17

   > ". . . for we must all stand before the judgment seat
   > of God. For it is written, as I live saith the Lord, to me
   > every knee shall bow, and every tongue shall confess to
   > God.

   > "So then each of us shall give account of himself to
   > God."        Romans 14:10–12

A person's life-style needs to be developed along
these four basic guide-lines. The specifics will vary and
situations will change, calling for flexibility which is not
inconsistent with conviction. In the end our objective
must be a way of life that:

ACTS APPROPRIATELY TO LIFE SITUATIONS
WITHIN THE CONTEXT OF THE FOUR
BASIC PRINCIPLES STATED ABOVE.

The question a father must ask is: "Am I demonstrating to our children appropriate actions and *how* to
determine what is right in different types of situations?
Also, am I helping our children think through for themselves an appropriate life-style for *their* circumstances?"

## DEMONSTRATING WHOLESOME
## INTERPERSONAL RELATIONSHIPS

A policeman told me he had apprehended a young adult for stealing from a farmer. In the course of their conversation the young man said, "The farmer had plenty and I had none and wanted some. So, why shouldn't I take what I want?"

The policeman was shocked by this attitude. Remonstrating with the fellow, he said, "Is that the way your mother taught you?" "Of course not," he replied, "But I don't believe her old way. That's just her idea. When I want something, why can't I have it? Especially when the other guy has plenty?"

The underlying philosophy expressed by the young man is the end result of today's overemphasis on the value of the individual versus the value of the group. The cry one hears on every hand says:

"Let me be free! Don't restrict me! I must have freedom to discover, develop and express my individual personhood!"

This idea is supported by many highly trained leaders in the field of behavioral science, educators and even religious leaders. It has been reflected in some of the major decisions by the U. S. Supreme Court. It underlies much of the uncertainty regarding the validity of laws that relate to human behavior, like the question of pornography, abortion, and nature of T. V. programs, open housing between the sexes on college campuses, etc.

The difficulty is rooted in the failure to recognize and accept the fact that there never is, nor can there ever be total freedom for any individual. As Paul put it:

149

"For none of us liveth to himself, and none dieth to himself."                                              Romans 14:7

Freedom, of necessity, is relative. There is a difference between inward freedom to be ourselves and outward freedom at the expense of others. Each person is a part of a group who belong in a variety of ways to each other — and all belong to God.

The dynamics, guide-lines, and appropriate expressions of inter-personal relationships are increasingly difficult to determine in the bewildering maze of today's society. While it may not be so difficult for the older generation, it certainly is a tough problem for many young people.

Never was it more important for fathers to demonstrate to their children what the Bible means by "loving one's neighbor as one's self." And this demonstration begins where we live most intimately — in the home.

Have you realized that the way your son treats his mother and his sisters was probably learned by observing how you treated his mother?

Do you really want your son to treat his wife the way you treat yours? Usually we reproduce what we are. What are you building into your children?

At the heart of interpersonal relationships is the value of people both as individuals and as groups. The law of love accepts the fact that my neighbor (wife, children or outside people) is equal in value to me — but a group of individuals is of more value than the individual alone.

Selfishness (the essence of sin), however, recognizes no law higher than that of personal interest.

"Let me have what I want when I want it — regardless of the well being of others or the law of God."

Your basic responsibility as a father is to demonstrate as well as teach your children in daily living how to apply the law of love in our complex society.

This demonstration must begin at home. Ask yourself how you are actually expressing the law of love, first toward your wife, then toward your children.

Do you treat them with consideration, thoughtfulness, respect?

How courteous are you in the family?

What does your tone of voice convey?

Your children will develop many of their ideas of marriage from what they observe in you in your daily life at home.

Do you have a high respect for the sanctity of the body and purity of sex, with it's rightness within the limits of marriage?

While we need to teach our children appropriateness of behavior toward the opposite sex, and instill high standards of conduct in dating, much of what they really learn will be more "caught than taught." Appropriate behavior toward the opposite sex, whether at the casual friendship level, in serious courtship, or in marriage — is rooted in the basic law of love. When this law is followed at these intimate levels, the other person will be better for having participated in the relationship. And *it is impossible to love genuinely without denying self and exercising self-control,* for love is the opposite of self-seeking.

How do you demonstrate self-denial and self-control in your relationships at home?

We also have interpersonal relationships outside the

home — with neighbors, people at work, the church, the community and the world at large. We have both friends *and* enemies. There are people with whom we are congenial and people with whom we have little in common. There is the fact of status: economically, educationally, professionally, and socially. Racial and cultural differences are also involved in relationships.

By the time most of us have become fathers, our relationship patterns are becoming fixed — almost second nature to us. Because of this many of us are not conscious of what we are really demonstrating to our children. That's why you need to take time periodically to ask yourself some serious questions:

Do I want my children to have my attitudes, and act like I do toward others?

Can I talk freely and wholesomely about this subject to my family? Do I?

Take time to explain to your children how you arrived at your attitudes and on what basis you justify them. Then help them think through some of their questions about the whole complex area of relationships in today's world.

Friends of ours lived in a lovely home in a middle-class subdivision. The wife and mother is an immaculate housekeeper, a delightful person, and an earnest Christian. The family has high moral standards and are looked up to in the community.

One day the mother came home from afternoon shopping to find that her high school son had brought home a ragged, dirty, unkept teen, whom he asked his mother to feed. The boy was a school dropout, on drugs, and had been met by her son at a local youth center. He explained to his mother that Jesus loved the boy and shouldn't they as Christians love him too? After God had some deep personal dealings with the mother, she became free in her spirit to show Christian love to the social "rejects" her son brought home.

In this case the son demonstrated the law of love to his mother, and became an example for the family to follow. But an example like this is not common. More often we communicate to our children that it's all right to love our neighbors in theory — but let's not feed them!

## DO YOU LEAD OR PREACH?

There's such a difference!

I grew up on the farm, although dad wasn't trained to be a farmer. He was a man of books, and when it came to farming he was great on consulting all the Department of Agriculture bulletins available on the wide range of topics related to farming.

Somewhere he had heard that the way to have a straight row when planting corn with a team of horses was to hold the reins tight and keep your eye fixed on an object at the other end of the row being planted.

I can still remember that awful day when I was given the job of planting a field of corn. Dad spent some time giving me a long lecture on the proper way to drive straight rows. It had to work. All I had to do was keep my eyes straight ahead on a post, tree, or something at the other end of the long row, hold the reins tight and keep the team moving. Then dad left, and I was on my own.

Later, when the corn came up it shouted to everyone how crooked the rows were. It really bothered me that dad never planted any rows himself. He read a theory from a book, told us kids how to do it, but never showed us how, personally.

Life could be so much more enjoyable if dads would work more *with* their children — making enjoyable jobs out of what could easily be boring chores. Like doing the yard together, or cleaning up the work center in the basement. You could even wash dishes with your girls!

One family stands out in my mind. We were living with them during two weeks of special meetings. First the husband awakened his wife with tea each morning. Then the mother woke each of their five children who spent the next thirty minutes in individual Bible study and prayer. While each was having his devotions privately, the parents were praying together. Those parents were leading, not preaching!

As someone has put it, "You can't lead where you haven't first followed." Don't ask your children to do what you aren't willing to do, and actually practice. Do you want them to be tidy? Make sure you lead the way by being tidy yourself. Do you have a rule about promptness at your house? Make sure you are prompt, and that you respond wholesomely and promptly when your wife calls you to meals.

Don't ask your children to break trail first; let them walk in your steps.

# 14

# Goals

**Targets for Training Your Children**

One sure way to hit the bull's-eye is to aim at nothing.

Most successful business or professional men have clearly defined goals for their work. These goals act as guidelines in determining activity priorities, use of time, and allocation of money and other resources.

What is necessary in the business world is too unusual in the home. But the family is in the greatest business in the world! If ever there was an area in life where goals are important, it's the home.

At the beginning of each year we review our family goals, make necessary changes, and plan our schedules accordingly. As the children have grown and our situation has changed, we have had to revise our goals and even change some drastically. This on-going practice has paid off over the years. It has helped to keep us flexible.

We have been able to adapt to changes more easily. It has helped to focus our prayers and faith, and to give a sound basis for decision-making.

While many families have general goals that relate to matters like buying a house, preparing the children for college, or planning for retirement; there is a lack in setting specific goals, especially in relation to the training of children at their various levels of growth.

What, specifically, are you seeking to accomplish in the training of your younger children?

How much serious thought and discussion have you given to it?

How much have you prayed about it?

Are you having difficulty agreeing on matters like:

— Discipline of the children?

— Their viewing of television?

— Their sleep habits? When they should go to bed and if they should go at a regular time?

— The children's chores around the home and how much responsibility they should carry?

In addition to the generally accepted objectives in the training of younger children — like learning to pick up after themselves, brushing their teeth, combing their hair, and having acceptable table manners — you and your wife need to think through, discuss, and agree on the absolute necessity of the one most important goal:

# THE DEVELOPMENT OF CHRISTIAN CHARACTER TRAITS IN EACH CHILD

This major goal can be broken down into several areas:

— Obedience.
— Honesty.
— Self-control.
— Right values.
— Practical love.
— Love of the Bible.
— An understanding of the way of salvation.
— Hopefully, an early acceptance of Christ as Savior.

Character is not something inborn, it must be developed over a period of time by repeated choices. These sub-goals are long range and you need to realize it will take time to develop each area.

To have these goals clearly in mind in order to work together on them can help tremendously in one major area of misunderstanding in family living.

As fathers, we often make an issue over incidentals. When a man wants to be the right kind of a father he often comes down too hard on specific matters which seem to him very important at the time. Parents tend to want adult behavior from their children long before the kids have grown up!

We had gotten a new car. Our daughter, age five, scratched her name on the fender with a rock! Wow! About all I could see was her name being scratched on all the cars up the street — to say nothing of the way I felt about having our own car ruined. The matter loomed like a mountain to me. The result was a case of horrible over-discipline, for which I had to ask forgiveness years later. About all I could think of at the time, however, was the importance of our daughter *never* doing such a thing again!

If I'd had a long-range goal about developing in my daughter an understanding and respect for the property of others, I would have seen the car-scratching incident for what it was — an incident. But I would have used the incident for teaching, not as the occasion for attempting to make sure she would never in the future scratch her name on any more cars!

A friend of ours had a large family of small children. He was an earnest Christian, wanting to rear his children properly. One day he said to me:

"Fred, I've come to see I'm not really training my children in obedience. I punish them for each wrong action. So instead of learning the *principle of obedience,* all they are learning is that they shouldn't do whatever it is they have done wrong."

"What do you mean, Hal?"

"Well, for example. The other day I told Jeff he shouldn't play in the yard because it was muddy. Later I learned he had played in the yard. So, I spanked him for playing in the yard and getting muddy. Another time he was told not to play with the newly born puppies. He did, so I punished him. Now I see that I should have dealt with him for *disobedience.* In chastening him, I had focused on the incident, rather than on the *principle of obedience.*

"Now I plan to make each incident an illustration of the larger long-range principle that I am seeking to teach. So, when I give a command, it will be reinforced by a reminder to *'obey daddy.'* And if the command is disobeyed, I'll deal with the child for disobedience rather than the specific incident."

This new thought paid off for Hal. We began to use it in our family, and it has worked for us. Life became much less complex. Dealing with the children became simpler and easier. We began to see the formation of Christian character in our children, rather than seeing them snarled in a mass of specific rules.

This helped us in the important issue of truthfulness. My wife and I felt very strongly about children telling the truth. We realized that we needed to see honesty (truthfulness) as a long-range goal for our children. In working with them, we used the incident of a lie to teach the truth, rather than making it a terrible crisis that gave the children the awful feeling *they* were "bad" for having told a lie.

I had to ask myself some questions.

"Why do my children lie?"

"Is there something in the way I relate to them that makes them lie?"

"If I weren't so rigid, could I get through to them more effectively and see more satisfying and lasting results?"

We changed our approach. We saw that we had frequently made it *unsafe* (to the child) for him to tell the truth. Jill helped me to see that my tone of voice and ultra serious manner could frighten a small child into a lie. Thinking back, I realized this was true in my childhood. Dad was very serious, both in his moods, tone of voice, and in his facial expression. There were plenty of times when I literally trembled at the thought of having

159

to tell the truth about something wrong that I had done. Lying was often done in self-defense. Of course that didn't make it right or justify it. I'm not proposing for a minute that we should condone untruthfulness; but what my father failed to do was to work with me, to *train* me in the character trait of truthfulness.

The Bible says: "Train up a child in the way he should go. . . ." Proverbs 22:6. All too often we only *tell* the child how he should go. But *telling is not training.* Of course telling is involved in training, but to train your child involves working with him in such a way that specific objectives are reached.

Naturally it's going to be next to impossible to train your children in areas where you have not developed yourself. But you don't have to wait until you're perfect before starting to work with your child. You can grow with him. Use some of your own struggles as opportunities to work with him. Take the area of self-control for example. Perhaps you never really learned it as a young person. Maybe you grew up uncontrolled, giving vent to your feelings in the easiest way that was safe for the moment. Now as a man you lose your temper, go into moods, or in other ways show your emotions and let your feelings rule you. Share with your child that this is an area where you *weren't* taught as a boy and now must learn as an adult to control yourself — which is much harder. Having talked it over with him, start working prayerfully on the issue together, making a challenge of the learning process. Self-control covers a wide range of behavior patterns: from crying softly when punished, talking pleasantly even when we don't feel like it, to curbing overly boisterous laughter when something funny

strikes us. Self-control is one of the fruits of the Holy
Spirit, and is essentially that work of God in the life by
which we become masters of ourselves instead of slaves to
ourselves.

As children mature their needs change. Foundations
are laid in early years of childhood. As they come into
their teen years our goals must suit their approaching
maturity. During adolescence and early adulthood we
need to continue to work on character development, only
now it will be even more necessary for the young person
to understand *why* these character traits are important.
We cannot force him to accept for himself those character values which we hold to be valid. But we can help him
think through the issues involved.

In order to be effective during this critical period,
you will need to be very understanding in three areas:

The normal developmental factors your teen is facing.

The normal problem areas with which he may be struggling.

The critical issues on which you should concentrate during
this period of your child's life.

It will help if you can share with him some of the
struggles you went through as a teen, and how you found
answers. Read some books on adolescent development.
Seek to identify with your teen. Don't make mountains
out of mole-hills, but avoid overlooking important issues.

One of the tragedies in many Christian homes is that
parents tend to relax spiritually about their children after
they have accepted Christ, or have dedicated their lives to
Christ in church or at camp. To relax is deadly when

these spiritual decisions were made at the child level. We fail to realize that the child is hardly aware of real life. For many, life awareness doesn't develop in a significant degree until middle or late adolescence, from age sixteen to nineteen. It is then that the *real* issues of life assume vital importance to the individual. It is in these areas that the emerging young adult has his battles. You as his father need to be aware of what is really going on. If ever your child needed the benefit of consistent believing and understanding prayer, open communication and wise counsel, it is during this period when the rudder of the young person's life is being set.

One of the most critical issues faced at this time is that of the Lordship of Jesus Christ. Up until early adulthood, the idea of Lordship has been for the most part a vague, poorly defined factor in life. But with the awakening to life issues, Christ's Lordship assumes dimensions that are both new and often frightening.

I can remember how vividly the thought of Lordship hit me when I was about sixteen. I was afraid if I surrendered to Christ, I'd never be allowed to get married. Or if I did I'd have to marry some old hag that a young fellow wouldn't be seen dead with! My thoughts were *completely* out-of-character with Christ!

You need to help your teen think through the implications of Christ being his Lord in the practical terms of friendships, life-goals, money, stewardship, dating behavior, general ethics, care of his body, and a host of other issues. He needs to see these issues for himself, but he will need to be helped to think them through, to be shown what the Bible has to say about them, and why. But most important of all *you must be faithful in prayer that the Holy Spirit will work* in his life in such depth that God-led life decisions will be made.

*The validity of a childhood decision for Christ is determined by life-choices made during adolescence and early adulthood.*

Sometimes a zealous father will make the mistake of trying to *push* (obviously or subtly) his teens into decisions involving commitment to full-time Christian service. This can be disastrous. While we need to speak of this as one of the areas to which God may direct a person, we are not wise in stressing this to the point of subconsciously pushing them in this direction.

We need rather to concentrate on showing young people —

— They need to be sensitive to God regardless of the vocation they may choose.

— They need to do all good they can in all walks of life.

— They will be accountable for the development and use of their gifts and potential in whatever they do.

In all of our training, particularly with teens, we need to demonstrate *by our example* the wholesomeness and satisfaction of a God-centered life.

Take the time right now and list your goals for training your children or your teens.

What limits have you set?

Discuss these with your wife.

What guidelines do you need to revise?

What practical steps are you both taking to reach them?

List steps you may have overlooked and will now begin to take.

# Part IV

Specifics

# 15

## Why Doesn't He Talk?

**The Problem of Communication**

I had spent three months in South America studying the problems of missionaries, and of course was eager to return home to my family. They were waiting excitedly as I walked through the airport arrival gate. After the initial joyous greetings, they burst out in a chorus with the request,

"Tell us about your trip!" But to their dismay the only thing I could say was one miserable sentence:

"I had a nice trip!"

It was as though I had punctured a balloon. Awkward silence made the moment painful until their mother came to the rescue with the words, "Daddy's tired from a long trip. Let's go and get his baggage. He'll tell us about everything tomorrow."

\* \* \* \* \*

"Mr. Renich, my husband is so clumsy when he tries to make love . . ."

167

"Have you ever talked to him about it?" I replied.

"Talked to him? He won't talk!"

\* \* \* \* \*

One of the frequent complaints a marriage coun-
sellor hears from wives is that their husbands won't talk.

Have you ever asked yourself how you rate in family
communications? Does your family really know what you
are thinking or how you feel?

Do you ever "whip them with silence?"

Is it safe for your wife or children to express themselves freely around you? Including telling you the truth
about you as they see it?

In spite of all the emphasis on communication today,
the multiplicity of words transmitted, and the growing
expressivism of society, adequate family communication
continues to be a rarity.

Ralph was a successful, popular salesman with his company.
Everyone at the office thought he was great. He was the life
of staff parties, dressed well, was good looking, and had an
uncanny way with prospects. The secretaries envied his
wife, thinking Ralph's home-life surely must be fun.

However, Ralph's marriage was in danger of falling apart.
Why? Because at home Ralph was more like a boring
Sphinx than an enjoyable companion. Night after night he
would sit in front of the TV replying to Laura's questions
with a grunt and ignoring his family's interests. Intimate
relationships were routine and mechanical. Meal times were
silent affairs interspersed with negative comments about the
food or occasional critical remarks to the children.

Ralph and Laura were hopelessly snarled in their lack of
communication. The more she tried to talk, the deeper he
seemed to retreat into a silence that could be felt. It was a

relief to her to have him leave for work in the morning and
she began to dread his coming home at night . . .

While we usually think of communication as talking,
there's so much more involved than words. And the fact
that lots of men are silent at home doesn't mean they
aren't communicating. The tragedy is, they are often
unaware of the degree to which they *are* communicating — *but negatively!*

Positive communication in the home involves sharing
yourself with your family. It's a mutual, loving, give-and-
take process. At its heart is love, providing the necessary
conditions of positive attitudes and wholesome family atmosphere.

Where genuine self-giving love is absent and/or
where selfishness is dominant in the home, true, positive
communication is impossible.

Jerry was a hard-working dedicated Christian worker. He
had a lovely wife and a large family. But he seemed to live
alone, within himself. His wife finally despaired of having
friends in because invariably as soon as the meal was over,
Jerry would retreat to his study, leaving his wife to entertain
the guests. Jerry's children grew up without any experience
of expressed affection from their father. They knew him
only as a stern, silent, brooding man. Jerry would have been
shocked had anyone suggested he didn't *really* love his family.

When you love your family you *will* work at entering
into the give and take of family interactions. This is a
process. It deepens, broadens and becomes increasingly
satisfying and rewarding as we let go of self interest and
become absorbed in the family's interests.

169

One evening we had a group over after dinner. Things went quite well for me for a time, then I visibly withdrew into silence. Although I didn't actually leave the group, I might just as well have.

Afterward, as Jill and I discussed the evening, she said to me:

"Honey, the trouble with you is that you love yourself too much. You are taken up with the things that interest you, and seem to have little interest in things that are important to other people. You are enthusiastic and talkative whenever the subject is of interest to you, but let the subject change to something outside the range of your personal interests and you withdraw so obviously it's painful."

I knew she was right, but of course didn't want to admit it. At the same time I was unhappy over my performance that evening, and I knew the party had been partially spoiled by my childish behavior. Jill continued:

"You know, dear, people love to have others show an interest in their interests. If you could only realize it, people themselves are intensely interesting. If you could learn to forget yourself and start showing an interest in the things others are interested in, you would discover that being with people can be lots of fun."

I'm very thankful for Jill's faithfulness to tell me the truth that evening. It marked the beginning of a change. Of course it took time and effort. But the results have been worth it.

Have you ever asked yourself to what degree you are consciously committed to being personally involved in the lives and interests of your family? Or is your own personal life more important?

It's interesting how you were able to communicate in a variety of ways when you were courting. And you didn't have to take a college course to learn to tell your sweetheart that she was the greatest! Who coached you on your proposal? Maybe you can't talk or say "sweet nothings" now, but you certainly could then!

The difference between then and now is that your love then was fresh, dynamic, and all absorbed in the thrill of relating to the one you loved. But somewhere along the way you began to get wrapped up in yourself and your interests. Self-love could have been predominant all along, but it was temporarily subordinated during courtship so you could "get" your girl. Maybe you never did really give *yourself* to her, but only *got her* for what she could satisfy in you. Like the groom I was trying to counsel blurted out, "Forget it, preacher, I want to hurry up and get married so I can have my bride."

And so, having "gotten" your girl, you relapsed more and more into living to please yourself, with little thought about the responsibility you have to share your inner life with that person who through marriage has become your "other self".

## COMMUNICATION CAN BE DEVELOPED

That's right, communication *can* be developed. But you have to work at it, and of course you won't really work at it unless you have an intense desire to communicate.

How can you get this desire?

Confess to God the sin of living within yourself.

Agree that your wife and children have a right to you. You belong to them just as much as they belong to you.

Part of the difficulty is that you tend to follow your feelings. It's easy to talk *if you feel like it.* But when you don't feel like talking you usually stay quiet. However, you are to live on the basis of what is *right* at the time rather than on the basis of how you *feel.*

To yield to feelings contrary to doing what is right is sin!

As you confess your sin of self-centeredness —

— Talk to God about the whole subject of sharing your life with your wife and children.

— Try to put yourself in their place.

— Imagine how they feel having a husband and father who never opens his heart to them — a man who remains essentially a stranger.

— Ask God to melt your heart, to enable you to *feel* the sin of your selfishness.

— Think back over the past and meditate on the times you have hurt members of your family by your silence or negative communication.

— Accept the fact that selfishness in relation to your family can be transformed by redeeming grace just as much as any other part of your life.

— Begin to look on the development of adequate communication as an exciting challenge — a battle to be won, or a prize to be gained.

*—Now, this minute —* start expecting God to
work a positive change in you.

*— Thank Him that He will —* AND FOLLOW
THROUGH BY LOOKING FOR WAYS
TO SHARE YOUR LIFE WITH YOUR
FAMILY!!

## HOW TO DEVELOP COMMUNICATION

*Recognize there are four basic ways people communicate.*
— Listening
— Speaking
— By Attitudes and Atmosphere
— Actions

Each of these is equally important, and you need to
accept the fact that you *are* communicating something to
your family *all the time* in one of these four ways.

*Make an honest appraisal of your communication.*

*How well do you listen?*

Do you really show interest in the things that your
wife and children are interested in? How?

When one of the children talks to you do you keep
on reading the paper? Are you usually too busy with your
own important affairs to give attention to your wife when
she tries to tell you something?

It takes time and effort to become a good listener. I
began to realize how easy it was for me to be preoccupied
with my own interests. I had to put my own concerns
aside *deliberately* and *choose* to listen to my wife or children.

There must be listening with love and understanding
as well as interest. This is what is so wonderful about

173

God. He listens to us with a full understanding of all that we are talking about, and He is *lovingly concerned.*

Be sure to listen for the *real* meaning your family is trying to communicate. Ask God to give you a sensitive, understanding heart. Watch jumping to conclusions. This is especially true with your teens. They often have difficulty expressing themselves clearly, and many times it seems to take them forever to verbalize what they want to say. It's easy for an adult to cut them off with a summary of what he thinks they are saying. How often I've done that, only to be told, "No dad, that isn't what I meant!" or "Please just listen until I'm through."

*Check up on your speaking.*

Ask yourself, "What do people really get from what I say?" Remember, it's not what you say that counts, but what the other person hears.

How do you know you are speaking lovingly as well as clearly?

When do you dominate the conversation, giving no time for others to talk and share their ideas?

What do others hear in the *tone* of your voice?

I was completely unaware of the fact that my tone of voice sounded angry to my children. I had to try to "hear myself" through their ears. We get so used to ourselves we don't realize *how* we sound to others. Check up on your tone of voice. Make a tape recording of some of your ordinary family conversation. Then listen to yourself. You'll probably have trouble believing it's really you doing the talking!

How clear is your speech and how adequate are the

174

words you use? Jill and I were having a hassle over something. Suddenly I remonstrated:

"But I told you exactly what I wanted."

"Yes," she replied, "and I did just what you told me."

"No you didn't. You didn't do at all what I told you."

"What exactly did you tell me?"

Patiently I explained.

"But darling, that's not what you said," replied Jill.

"But it's what I meant!"

"Then why didn't you say what you meant? I'm no mind reader, you know!!"

What you want to say may be very clear in your own mind. But you have to say *it in words that convey to the other person what you are thinking.*

Ask yourself another question. *What does your attitude convey to people?*

How does it set them free in spirit or how does it tie them in knots?

Attitudes really communicate — especially in the family where life is lived so closely and intimately. You can't hide from your family. When you have a negative attitude toward one member of the family, they can't help but know it right away. Until God began dealing with me about it, I'd whip my family by nursing a poor attitude. Inevitably it would show in my speech by short precise statements or tension in my voice. This put the family on edge because they knew dad was unhappy about something.

When this happens, there's only one thing to do. Get the matter out in the open and clear it up. We're a lot better about this than we used to be. And our family is much more free.

175

*Specifics*

Here are some words that describe *quality* of communication. Check which ones fit you:

| | |
|---|---|
| Lovingly honest | Evasive or untrue |
| Open | Closed |
| Satisfying to others | Critical and negative |
| Interesting | Belittling |
| Clear | Inadequate |
| Encouraging | Uninteresting |
| Pleasant | Unpleasant |

Ask yourself what your actions communicate to those around you.

How is your family better because of your involvement with them?

How do you encourage good communication in your home, or how do you hinder it?

When do your wife and children feel free to be honest and open around you? *How can you tell you make it safe for them to tell you the truth* ABOUT *you as they see it or feel it?* Children and many wives learn early in the game that it's wise to speak carefully around dad.

We had a family conference around our dinner table one evening. We all agreed we'd try to be open and honest with each other. A week or so later Rick came into my study:

"Dad, did we agree we were going to be open and honest around here?"

"That's right."

"Are you sure?"

"Yep."

"Does it still hold?"

"Yes sir," I replied.

"O.K. I just wanted to make sure, because I've got something to say."

Whereupon my son proceeded to tell me where he felt I had missed the boat regarding a certain matter. But he wanted to make sure at the outset that it was *safe* to express himself!

It's tragic how many teens have learned that the safe way is to tell their parents what the parents want to hear, or else to cover up the truth with some vague generalities. Often the fault lies with us husbands and fathers. We've failed to make our families *feel* it's safe for them to tell us the truth, especially about us.

After you have an overall picture of what your communication is like, and feel you can look at the picture objectively — *Try to identify your hangups.*

Make a list of the things *in others* that irritate you or make you freeze. Maybe it's a certain tone in your wife's voice, or some mannerism in one of your children. We need to be honest about how others in the family affect our own ability to communicate. List these and other hindrances to communication in your family as you see them. Here's a sample list:

Too busy.
Too much TV
Marcy dominates every conversation.
Maybe I'm prejudiced.
Jack's sullen silence turns me off.
I'm afraid I'll seem dumb or stupid.
I'm not interested in what my wife wants to talk about.
My wife has all the answers. When she's spoken there's
  nothing more to say.

177

She's always right.

Whenever we try to talk it turns into an argument.

She says I'm stubborn and opinionated.

I'm often in no mood to talk, then I'm accused of being a bore.

The family isn't interested in the things that are important to me.

I have to talk all day at work, so I'd just like to be quiet and relaxed when I'm home.

The kids say I preach at them whenever I talk. I think they ought to be willing to take a little advice now and then.

When I want to talk my wife is busy with other things, and by the time she's finished I'm either out of the notion or else too tired and want to go to sleep.

Whenever anyone talks at our house it sounds like they're chipping at someone. Everyone is critical or sarcastic.

*Pray about each of the items on your list.* Ask God to show you the deeper problem or the cause for the hindrance. Which ones are due to something in you that you need to change? Think through how you can change and work on improving.

I realized that part of the problem in our home was due to my tendency to be overly serious. I began to see that God wanted me to have a "song" in my voice and a brightness in my spirit that would make people want to be around me. It dawned on me that if I'd let God manage life's problems, I wouldn't need to brood over them, and I could live life with a much lighter touch.

The next step was for me deliberately to turn my mind off my problems. I learned to give them to God and start singing — inwardly if not audibly, especially on my way home.

178

*Study the following verses and ask God how to apply them
in your own circumstances:*

"Ye offspring of vipers, how can ye, being evil, speak good
things? for out of the abundance of the heart the mouth
speaketh. And I say unto you, that every idle word that men
shall speak, they shall give account thereof in the day of
judgment. For by thy words thou shalt be justified, and by
thy words thou shalt be condemned."

Matthew 12:34,36,37

"Let no corrupt speech proceed out of your mouth, but
such as is good for edifying as the need may be, that it may
give grace to them that hear. Let all bitterness, and wrath,
and anger, and clamor, and railing, be put away from you,
with all malice: and be ye kind one to another, tenderhear-
ted, forgiving each other, even as God also in Christ forgave
you."

Ephesians 4:29,31,32

"And be not drunken with wine, wherein is riot, but be
filled with the Spirit; speaking one to another in psalms and
hymns and spiritual songs, singing and making melody in
your heart to the Lord."

Ephesians 5:18,19

"Let your speech be always with grace, seasoned with salt,
that ye may know how ye ought to answer each one."

Colossians 4:6

"And the Lord's servant must not strive, but be gentle to-
wards all, apt to teach, forbearing, in meekness correcting
them that oppose themselves:

II Timothy 2:24, 25

"Put them in mind . . . to speak evil of no man, not to be
contentious, to be gentle, showing meekness toward all
men."

Titus 3:1,2

". . . If any stumbleth not in word, the same is a perfect
man, able to bridle the whole body also . . . So the tongue
also is a little member, and boasteth great things. Behold

how much wood is kindled by how small a fire! And the
tongue is a fire: the world of iniquity among our members is
the tongue, which defileth the whole body, and setteth on
fire the wheel of nature, and is set on fire by hell . . . but
the tongue can no man tame; it is a restless evil, it is full of
deadly poison. Therewith bless we the Lord and Father;
and therewith curse we men, who are made after the like-
ness of God: out of the same mouth cometh forth blessing
and cursing . . . who is wise and understanding among
you? Let him show by his good life his works in meekness of
wisdom. But if ye have bitter jealousy and faction in your
heart, glory not and lie not against the truth. This wisdom is
not a wisdom that cometh down from above, but is earthly,
sensual, devilish. For where jealousy and faction are, there
is confusion and every vile deed. But the wisdom that is
from above is first pure, then peaceable, gentle, easy to be
entreated, full of mercy and good fruits, without variance,
without hypocrisy. And the fruit of righteousness is sown in
peace for them that make peace."

James 3:2,5,6,8,9,10,13–18

"For he that would love life and see good days, let him
refrain his tongue from evil, and his lips that they speak no
guile: And let him turn away from evil, and do good; let
him seek peace, and pursue it."          I Peter 3:10,11

*Choose one or two hindrances in which the whole family is
involved,* and try to discuss them freely and objectively.
Try to have the family agree that you all will help each
other develop more wholesome communication.

*Select one or two communication objectives and work on
them.* You can't do everything at once. Your communication patterns have developed over a period of
time. It will take time to change them.

Jill and I realized we needed a more cheerful atmosphere at the breakfast table, with pleasant conversation that would provide pleasant memories for the children as they left for school. As we faced the issue we recognized that the root problem was quite simple — one of us was a "slow starter" who needed more time to "come alive" in the morning. In addition to prayer and making sure our attitudes were right, we found that having coffee in bed helped tremendously! If someone at your house has trouble being cheerful at breakfast, maybe something as simple as a brisk shower, a cup of coffee, or a short walk outside will help get their "motor" going.

My work involved talking to people all day. When I got home I wanted quiet and seclusion. Jill recognized this and suggested I needed a "transition time" from my world of work to the world of the family. She deliberately planned things so we could have fifteen to thirty minutes of quiet together over cups of tea before dinner and the evening's family activities. It helped immensely.

Are you willing to work at developing better communication with your family? When you really love them you will. Remember, family communication is simply sharing yourselves with each other in ways that are understood and appreciated by each other.

Most communication breakdowns occur because of default. We tend to follow our inclinations and take the path of least resistance, instead of working steadily and consistently toward reasonable and clearly defined goals.

181

*Specifics*

*Set your goals today — and start working on them now!*
— What will you change in *your* communication?
— What *hindrances* to communication will you work on?
— What hindrance to communication will you work on *as a family?*

# 16

# Is That All Men Think About?

## Sex *Is* a Part of Marriage

Karin was an attractive, intelligent young wife whose husband was moving up the corporate ladder toward success in his chosen field. They were active in their church, professed to be dedicated Christians, had a modest but lovely home and two delightful children. Karin had called for a counselling appointment, and was seated in my office:

"Mr. Renich, everyone thinks my husband Todd is the greatest, and I used to think so too. But I'm becoming more and more resentful toward him. We used to enjoy being together. Love-making was fun. Todd was considerate, thoughtful and understanding. But lately all that has changed. He comes home and hardly says a word. He is critical and moody. And as for our love-relationship, forget it!"

"Could you explain that last statement a little, Karin?" I requested.

"Well, time and again he comes home acting like a bear. He psychologically beats me black and blue or else treats me like a rug under his feet. Then when we go to bed, five minutes before he goes to sleep, he gets all sweet and loving and it's obvious he wants sex. He has no consideration for me and leaves me tighter than a drum and ready to climb the walls, while he turns over and goes blissfully off to sleep.

"Mr. Renich, is sex all men think about when they think about love?"

"Karin, I don't think you really understand men. Don't get me wrong. I'm not about to excuse Todd or justify what he's doing. The tragedy is that he's probably only dimly aware of how much he is hurting you. But probably Todd is far from happy either. In fact, he may be pretty miserable.

"I wouldn't say sex is *all* men think about when they think about love. But sex *is* for a man a big part of the package. For most men, sex is included when they think about love. The problem is they can't understand why their wives don't feel the same way.

"Let's look at the broader picture.

"Men and women function differently. While we know this in our heads, we don't recognize it practically at the level of day by day living.

"Todd is dead sure he loves you with everything he has. Why else do you think he's slaving away to get to the top in his field? Sure, I know he gets a big ego boost everytime he gets a promotion, and status means a lot to him. But *in his own mind* he's doing all of this for you. He equates his work and his drive toward success with his love for you. A man thinks of love largely as *deeds*. Being a good provider is to a man an obvious way of loving.

"But it may not dawn on Todd you don't see it that way. Don't you really take him for granted too? Todd is successful. He subconsciously thinks that proves his love. You take all this for granted. Doesn't every *decent* husband provide for his wife? But to you that's not love! Love for you is a lot more, including romantic emotion!

"If Todd would start the day with some sweet nothings about how wonderful you are,

— express appreciation for your breakfast.
— show some thoughtful concern about your day,
— greet you warmly and affectionately when he comes home,
— ask what he could do to help

and in various ways tell you how lucky he is to have you as his wife — well, it could be that you might even *want* his love-making at night! Especially if he was more interested in satisfying you sexually than in simply getting what he wanted then going off to sleep."

"You know, Mr. Renich, I think you're right. Like I said, there used to be times when Todd has done that. And frankly I loved our intimate times together. Then the sex part of loving seemed so right — like an exciting and beautiful experience of total oneness. But the way it's been recently — ugh! I feel like I'm just being used for his satisfaction. There's no love to it, and it's repulsive."

"Could it be, Karin, that you feel maybe Todd is in love with his job, and that he's rejected you as a person, so that you've been relegated to the level of a servant? Someone who is important to him only to the extent that you provide satisfaction for a variety of needs, like — food, a clean house, cared-for children, and a bed-mate?

"Your problem is an everyday occurrence in thousands of good Christian homes! But its roots lie in our failure to work at building bridges over the chasms that mark our differences. Without a bridge, you look at Todd from your side, your own perspective, and he looks at you through his thoughts and feelings. Neither of you has learned to accept the other *as you are* or to look at your relationship through the other person's eyes.

"You *can* do this only as you choose lovingly to tell each other how you really feel — to open your hearts to each other. When you go day after day without being honest with each other, distorted ideas of the other person begin to form in your own minds. You begin to suspect each other's motives, and you find yourselves reading evil into even the good the other person tries to do!

"Don't kid yourself, Karin. Todd isn't really satisfied with just physical sex. Sure he goes off to sleep after having had intercourse. But that doesn't mean he's satisfied.

"The fact is, for a man sex serves as an emotional and physical release-valve. A man *can* be tired as a dog, mad as a hornet, frustrated and uptight about life, and this tension often can be released through intercourse. Furthermore a man is stimulated sexually in bed, and by touch. Besides a husband feels his wife belongs to him. What's more, he feels that sexual involvement with his wife is perfectly pure, God-ordained and right."

"At this point, Karin, he doesn't think the way a woman thinks. A man experiences intense feelings of love in the act of intercourse. Here his tensions are released, many problems are resolved or at least reduced, and sleep is the next logical step.

"But while a man *seems* to be satisfied just with physical sex, he really isn't. There is a deeper release of emotion, and a deeper kind of satisfaction which a husband really wants to experience. It occurs when he knows his wife is giving herself to him in unreserved love, that he is giving her pleasure

186

in the act of sex, and when their mutual abandonment to each other is an expression of their total oneness."

\* \* \* \* \*

Underneath the problem Karin shared with me was a lack of understanding by both Karin and Todd of the fundamental differences between men and women regarding sex, its place in marriage, and the dynamics related to it. But the complaint of many wives is that their husbands won't read books on the subject, while at the same time the wives seem to feel that to discuss their feelings about sex with their husbands would destroy something romantic.

Let's look for a minute at what the Bible says in I Corinthians 7:3–5 L.B.:

> The man should give his wife all that is her right as a married woman, and the wife should do the same for her husband: for a girl who marries no longer has full right to her own body, for her husband then has his rights to it, too; and in the same way the husband no longer has full right to his own body, for it belongs also to his wife. So do not refuse these rights to each other . . ." \*

From these verses it is very plain that you and I as husbands have the responsibility to do our best to meet the sexual and emotional needs of our wives. But in seeking to meet those needs, we need to be sure we understand them from our wife's point of view, just as she needs to try to understand our needs from our point of view.

If this kind of mutual understanding is going to de-

---

\* Taylor, Kenneth, *The Living Bible,* Wheaton, Illinois, Tyndale House Publishers, 1972. Used by permission.

velop between you and your wife, you as the husband *must* make sure there is free and open communication between you. While it will help for both of you to read books * on this subject, nothing can take the place of open and free communication. The books can give general guidelines, but people are too distinctly individual, and couples vary too much in their individuality for a book to have all the answers.

It's easy for a man to get wrapped up in the demands and challenge of a job — or to get mired down in its monotony and boredom. Some men assume that being a good provider is an adequate expression of love. Men tend to assume their wives get just as excited physically as they do just by sight and proximity in the bed-room, but many don't. It is difficult for a man to realize that problems, tensions, a bad day or worry *unfit* a woman emotionally for intimacy. For men the opposite is more often true.

It is very important a husband provide for his wife an emotional climate which prepares her for love-making. Her preparation may come in taking time to talk out her frustrations and sensing your tender acceptance of her. The pain of an argument which freezes a woman can be thawed by an understanding apology. She needs to feel you love *her* and need *her* and that she as a person is important to you. Once the climate is warmed and a husband takes time for love-play many wives become most responsive.

* Miles, Herbert J., *Sexual Happiness in Marriage,* Grand Rapids, The Zondervan Publishing House, 1967.

* LaHaye, Tim and Beverly, *The Act of Marriage,* Grand Rapids, The Zondervan Publishing Corporation, 1976.

Ask yourself some questions:

How freely do you and your wife discuss your intimate relationships? What are her troubled areas? What makes her touchy?

Are you open and honest with each other, or do either of you hide your true feelings? Does your wife freely tell you the truth about how she really feels? *How do you know?*

Have you explained patiently and lovingly how *you* feel about sex? Do you express *in words* your need for your wife, or do you assume she knows, then when she doesn't respond as though she knew, you get upset?

Do you ever clam up and turn inwardly resentful when your wife fails to respond to your subtle suggestions that you would like to have intercourse?

Do you take time for love-play? Do you ask your wife to tell you how she feels about intimate relationships including what she likes you to do, or what you like her to do before and during intercourse?

Do you think of sexual involvement in your marriage as a desirable experience that stands pretty much alone, or do you think of it as part of a much wider love-relationship with your wife? How do you express that wider love-relationship? Does she feel that you express genuine love in a variety of ways and at times when there is no suggestion of sexual intimacy?

Are you able freely and wholesomely to talk through areas where you may have differences? Such as use and methods of birth control? Frequency of intercourse? Times, places, and methods? Who initiates? Various actions in foreplay? Actions and ways that are offensive to either of you?

It is imperative that you and your wife develop an increasingly satisfying, enjoyable and harmonious sex life.

But sometimes men can be terrific lovers and forget how important it is to work on the wider areas of marriage!

The physical and emotional elements in marriage are important and very central. But sex is not everything. When a man's wife gives her body to him in physical intimacy, she subconsciously wants that giving to be related to feelings of love, admiration, respect, implicit confidence, and maybe even pride. A husband cannot demand respect and admiration. Nor can he demand confidence from another. He must win these. Your goal should be to grow as a person so that your wife will deepen in her admiration and respect for you.

It's pathetic when a woman shares with her counselor that her husband is a terrific sex partner — everything a woman could want at that level, but that he's inadequate as a husband, father or life companion. A wife wants so much more from her husband than love-making with its caresses and even sex. She wants a man she can look up to, work with, admire, respect, trust, and unhesitatingly follow.

It will help if you can see the delights of intimacy in the context of a much wider horizon. Think of your marriage as the wonder of you two people being joined together for the purpose of fulfilling the will of God with all your varied abilities and gifts.

For every couple there is a God-ordained purpose in life so much greater than satisfying personal desire. When we make personal satisfaction our goal, we shrivel as people. God made us for something much higher and greater! *As important as love-making is, and as exciting and satisfying as sexual intimacy can be, these are not to be ends in themselves, or the reasons for marriage.* God planned that emotional and physical intimacy in mutually satisfying sex should serve as a unifying bond between a married couple, and a means toward a greater end — to fulfill God's reason for two people made one through marriage.

As you and your wife grow together in your oneness, you will be proportionately free and able to accomplish God's purpose for your creation and redemption.

# 17

# Do You Call That a Bargain?

## Conflicts over Values

"Oh honey, look at the cute dress I got on sale at Barker's!"

"How much?"

"It was only half-price. Believe me, it's a real bargain."

"Sally, do you call *that* thing a dress? Why there's nothing to it — and you paid good money for that ugly bag? Style? A model T has more style than that piece of junk."

When would she ever begin to see that you had to get something worthwhile for your money? And besides, they had so little to live on. Once more Sally had blown their meager bit on, of all things, a dress that wasn't even worth carrying home. After all, dresses should look nice as well as be in style. But this thing — he wouldn't wish it off on his worst enemy.

The argument that developed between Chuck and Sally killed all the joy Sally had anticipated from wearing her stunning new dress — and Chuck's frustration over his wife's use of money went several notches deeper.

Nobody had explained to either Chuck or Sally that men and women often have totally different value systems. It's hard enough to harmonize differences in values when we *know* they are legitimate, but to avoid conflict when we don't know they exist is nearly impossible.

Seldom do any two people look at life alike, much less when a man and a woman are involved. Men tend to be more utilitarian, concerned with things like performance, durability, practicality and serviceability. Women tend to value the aesthetic factors such as color, appearance and feel. In looking at a house, men would look at the foundation, condition of the plumbing and the future resale value. A woman would probably think more of its style, the decor and general appearance and appeal.

The problem is we think of our own value system as "right," and automatically assume the other person feels the same way about *our* viewpoint. If she differs *she's* wrong!

I've always had a "thing" about balancing my checkbook — even to sitting up half the night trying to find a missing penny. Of course, I was "right" in my value system. "Isn't accuracy next to godliness?" I thought.

Jill looks at it differently. "Why lose sleep over a paltry penny?"

My trouble was that I saw her viewpoint as *wrong* and mine as *right*. To me the penny represented a principle. And anyone worth his salt will die for his principles, or so I thought.

193

*Specifics*

Do you get upset over things your wife does without stopping to ask yourself *why* she does them? You may need to spend time honestly sharing your sense of values with each other. This is important even when there isn't conflict between you. Absence of conflict doesn't mean you understand and appreciate each other's point of view.

The Penningtons were Christian farmers. Life was hard and finances always seemed inadequate. While they didn't quarrel over money, there was an obvious imbalance in how it was used. Mr. Pennington appeared to pay little attention to his wife's desire to keep the home and yard attractive. She did well with what little he gave her for maintenance of the home. But *he* always had the latest in dairy equipment and gadgetry for the farm. It was pathetic how the aesthetic needs of his wife were unmet because they weren't part of her husband's value system.

\* \* \* \* \*

Jason was so proud of his new home. It was engineered to the hilt and would stand like the Rock of Gibralter. But when it was completed he seemed to be unaware of what was important to Judy. She dreamed of attractive decor, suitable furnishings, pleasant landscaping and lovely flower borders. It was hard and not very enjoyable to plant the garden alone. In their case they didn't have open conflict. They rather lived in the aloneness of their individual value worlds.

Values should be harmonized, but *they don't need to be identical.* The utilitarian and the enjoyable can be like two sides of the same coin. A garment can be both stylish and serviceable. A meal can be substantial and attractively served.

194

Your wife needs the practicality of your values, but you need the added dimension of her feminine sensitivities.

Remember, differences between people can be assets — but that depends on how you look at them! If you assume your values are "right" then everything your wife does that violates your values will be "wrong." And of course, for a conscientious person, there can be no "give" when dealing with issues that are "right" or "wrong".

How can you harmonize differences?

You must begin by believing your wife wants to do what is right, just as she must believe you are committed to the right.

With this acceptance of each other's motives, be willing to be honest with each other in *sharing and listening* to your respective individual points of view.

It took quite a while for me to drop my rigid "My mind's made up: don't confuse me with the facts" attitude. I had a sneaking notion Jill might be right, and *I* didn't want to be proven wrong. One day we had a talk about my hangup over her method of keeping accounts. Patiently she explained how she felt about spending hours worrying over a lost penny or two.

When I became *really willing to listen* I saw she was right. Did this mean that I dropped my way and adopted hers? In this instance, no. But it did mean I stopped bugging her. She became free to handle her accounts *her* way, while I continued to handle mine as I always had.

It was important that our differences in value systems stopped being an occasion for conflict. When I dropped my rigidity, Jill became free. We found ourselves drawn closer together as well as better people through our understanding and acceptance of each other. And funny thing, she's not been losing as many pennies!

Think through your own value system to know how you feel about life in its various components. Ask yourself questions like — "How come I feel strongly about this?" or "Why doesn't that type of thing bother me?" Maybe people at your house have to eat everything on their plates because you were trained that way as a child. And now you get upset because your wife doesn't have a conscience about the clean plate club!

Encourage your wife to think through her value system and ask herself the same questions.

Make a list of areas of conflict. Maybe she's a saver and you feel money is more for spending. Perhaps you are work-centered and she feels it's more important to have people around. Possibly you feel it's imperative that the children make good grades while she may feel it's more important for them to adjust happily to life at school than to be overly concerned about making top marks.

Take time to talk over each area of conflict. Remember you're seeking for understanding and harmony, not evaluation, self-justification or judgment of the other person. This will necessitate both of you remaining objective. If either of you begins to get emotionally involved or critical and accusing, drop the subject and move to something else, or agree to try at a later date.

If you are the sensitive one, ask yourself why? Are you insecure? Are you fearful that your wife's point of view might have validity? Do you want what is best for the family *regardless of whose point of view is followed?* Many conflicts erupt because the husband feels threatened by his wife's intuitive perception. If she sees some issues more clearly than you, be thankful. God gave her to you to be your helper, *where you need* her as well as where you *want* her help.

If your wife gets defensive or touchy, could it be that you were trying to "prove your point?" Are you communicating to her a negative and judgmental attitude toward her point of view? Does she feel *personally* threatened?

Could it be important for the children to be *both* well adjusted at school and still aim at reasonably good grades? It may not be an either/or!

So you're work-centered, while she wants to be more involved socially. Where is the happy medium? Some men enjoy work, while others are work centered because they are uncomfortable with people socially. But you need people, and if your wife enjoys them be glad. God gave her to you to help you learn to enjoy them with her. Work toward mutual understanding, living *and* working as a team, and enjoying the comradeship of life together.

You need to accept each other's general value system and work out mutually satisfying applications of these to daily life. It is especially important for you to find genuine agreement about the use and management of money.

Tim believed in the "common purse" idea for his family. All money the family earned went into the purse, and he managed it. This arrangement suited him fine, but he couldn't understand why his wife and children needed to have money of their own for which they didn't need to give an account. Bonnie felt it demeaning to ask her husband for

Specifics

money every time she wanted something personal. Her only recourse was to hide her personal gift money and use it sparingly. The same was true of the children. Instead of money being a means toward happiness and harmony, it was a cause of friction, frustration, deceit and unhappiness.

Very seldom do two people see money or its management the same way. Nor are we equal in our ability to acquire it and use it. Some people are adept at earning money, but hopeless as managers of what they earn. Then there are those who feel that the family finances are strictly the husband's domain. Some men feel their manhood is threatened if they let their wives manage the family budget.

God has given each of us varied abilities. It was evidently His plan that the totality of the gifts entrusted to a married couple would be adequate for that couple to fulfill the will of God for them.

*These gifts are your family's assets.* As leader in your home it is your responsibility to see that these assets are used wisely and fully for the common good. Look at your family finances this way. Is your wife a good manager? Then let her handle the finances; only keep things open and clear between you. Delegating this area of responsibility to your wife doesn't make you less a man, nor does it imply that she is assuming a dominant role. Remember, if you are an insecure husband, handling the money (when your wife can do it better) won't resolve your insecurity! See her money-manager role as an asset to *you.* Now you are released from burdensome responsibility enabling you to get on with other jobs for which you are better suited.

What a delight when husband and wife pool their

198

abilities. And to use them wisely promotes the well-being and happiness of the family and helps achieve their mutual life goals.

Assignment:

1. Study Proverbs 31:10–31
2. In what ways does your attitude toward your wife's value system set her free inwardly to develop and use her abilities so that you are a better man because of her? (see verses 11, 12, and 23.)

# 18

# Raindrops!

## Her Emotions May Confuse You

"Now *why* does she act like that? All I did was ask her what she'd been doing all day. She acts like I'm accusing her of loafing, when I was trying to show interest in *her* day's activities and wanted some facts!"

\* \* \* \* \*

"Honey, I didn't mean it the way you seem to have taken it. I just said the place needed a good cleaning. You act like I said *you* were a no good wife."

\* \* \* \* \*

"Relax dear, it's O.K. Why make such a big deal out of it? So I forgot it's our anniversary. We're still married aren't we? And together. And tomorrows will come and we have each other. Why get so upset over such a little thing?"

\* \* \* \* \*

"Look, sweetheart, staying up won't get Jim home any sooner. Why not relax and get some sleep."

\* \* \* \* \*

"Please darling, do you *have* to cry just because I said the steak was overdone? I wasn't accusing you. I was just stating a fact. Good grief! A fellow can't say anything around here without bringing on a cloudburst."

\* \* \* \* \*

"O.K., O.K. If that will make you feel better we'll go visit your mother. I'm not sure the boss will give me brownie points for taking the time off, but I guess he won't fire me."

\* \* \* \* \*

"Look, I just suggested you could take the taxi to the airport. It *doesn't* meant I don't love you. And it doesn't help for you to get so upset over the idea. I'd love to take you personally, but the boss made it clear we were *not* to be late for the sales meeting. And if I drive you to the airport I'm sure to be late! Why can't women understand simple facts?"

\* \* \* \* \*

Emotions!
Weeping!
Tears!
Do they make you feel uncomfortable?

If so, you're pretty normal. A lot of men have a hard time trying to understand women and their emotions. So, if you're saying, "How can I figure her out?" remember you belong to a very large club of mystified husbands!

However to keep the record straight, our wives have an equally tough time figuring out us husbands! And we're probably as unpredictable to them as they are to us.

Whether you do or don't understand your wife is not the most important issue. Do you *really* accept her? Ac-

201

ceptance must precede understanding. And acceptance must be wholehearted, positive, and without an attitude that she's wrong to be the way she is.

I don't think our wives expect us to understand *how* they function emotionally, but they do want us to be aware of their feelings, to be gentle, considerate and to appreciate them in their sometimes unpredictable expressions of emotion.

Part of the difficulty is that many men look on emotion as a sign of weakness. Maybe you can remember your playmates at school or your father shaming you with the cruel words, "Cry-baby." I can remember how often as a boy I fought to keep the tears back because I wanted to act like a man! Background, conditioning, cultural values, and the nature of a man's world of work all tend to put a premium on being non-emotional, factual and objective. The net result may be an insensitivity to emotion as a valid God-given dynamic in life.

Your wife doesn't want *you* to be weak. She appreciates the fact that little things don't get you all unstrung. Your quiet composure and unruffled objectivity are reassuring to her and provide for her more volatile nature a sense of security. But she does want you to try to understand her feelings. So many wives feel their husbands are insensitive, hard and just tolerant of their emotion.

Remember, God commands us to show emotion.

Study the following Bible passages:

"Don't just pretend that you love others: really love them. Hate what is wrong. Stand on the side of the good. Love each other with brotherly affection and take delight in honoring each other. Never be lazy in your work, but serve the Lord enthusiastically.

202

Be glad for all God is planning for you. Be patient in trouble, and prayerful always. When God's children are in need, you be the one to help them out. And get into the habit of inviting guests home for dinner or, if they need lodging, for the night. If someone mistreats you because you are a Christian, don't curse him; pray that God will bless him. When others are happy, be happy with them. If they are sad, share their sorrow. Work happily together. Don't try to act big. Don't try to get into the good graces of important people but enjoy the company of ordinary folks. And don't think you know it all!     Romans 12:9–16 L.B.*

"Don't forget about those in jail, suffer with them as though you were there yourself. Share the sorrow of those being mistreated, for you know what they are going through."

Hebrews 13:3 L.B.*

"And did I not weep for those in trouble? Wasn't I deeply grieved for the needy?"     Job 30:25 L.B.*

"I do them good, but they return me harm. I am sinking down to death. When they were ill, I mourned before the Lord in sackcloth, asking him to make them well; I refused to eat; I prayed for them with utmost earnestness, but God did not listen. I went about sadly as though it were my mother, friend or brother who was sick and nearing death."

Psalms 35:12–14 L.B.*

In each of these passages there is an emotional identification with other people. We are not isolated islands in a sea of humanity — we are a part of a large family that has many varied and deep feelings. And the Bible teaches that we must identify in our feelings with those around

* Taylor, Kenneth, *The Living Bible,* Wheaton, Illinois, Tyndale House Publishers, 1971. (Used with permission.)

us. Close to every husband is his wife, and he must identify with her in her feelings.

But the real issue is not that men don't understand
women and vice versa. Nor is it that men function differently than women. There is a deeper underlying issue
which must be faced squarely if you are going to relate
maturely and wholesomely to your wife as a person who
expresses her personhood differently than you do. This
deeper issue concerns you and the degree to which your
experience of God as a person is genuine and growing.

Many authorities are saying that the emotional dynamics of men are the product of cultural conditioning.
The idea being that right from the beginning a boy is
pressured to suppress emotion, to develop a kind of psychological callous to life, to become objective in his out-
look, and to varying degrees hard-nosed and thick
skinned.

It is felt by many, conversely, that our culture is responsible for the degree to which women may be more
volatile and unpredictable emotionally, less objective,
more emotionally sensitive and more easily moved to
tears. After all, aren't they treated differently than boys
right from birth? They are expected to be "little ladies."
Mothers don't like their daughters climbing trees, playing
cops and robbers, and in general becoming the neighborhood "tomboy."

There are movements in society today that are attempting to eliminate what is regarded as arbitrarily conceived and imposed cultural distinctives.

With full recognition of the obvious fact that the traditional western attitudes toward male and female roles
may account for *some* of the behavioral differences evi-

dent between men and women, the answer to the deeper problem will not be found in attacking the culture. Were we to succeed in eliminating the superficial distinctions between men and women by developing a new unisex culture we would *still* have the problem of basic difference.

The heart of *both* traditional culture and the new culture envisioned by women's liberationists is the same: the development and establishment in every person of a strong spirit of independence. Our traditional attitude has been that the male is the strong, independent, self-sufficient element in society, and that the female is the dependent element. The revolutionaries are saying, "Not so — rather *both male and female* are equally independent, self-sufficient and strong."

Both views are in direct conflict with the eternal fact that men as well as women are dependent beings and the kingdom of God is therefore entered into only by those who have turned from independence and self-sufficiency of spirit to that of dependence. This is what Jesus meant when He said:

> ". . . Except ye turn, and become as little children, you shall in no wise enter into the Kingdom of heaven. Whosoever therefore shall humble himself as this little child, the same is the greatest in the Kingdom of heaven."
>
> Matthew 18:3,4

The problems you and I may have accepting our wives as they are, being aware of their sensitivities and appreciating their feelings will not be solved either by an intellectual understanding of *what* may have made them that way, nor by a fundamental change in their status and role in society. It will be resolved *only by a drastic change in our heart-attitude toward people.*

Many wives suffer deeply because of the hard, abrupt, unfeeling attitude of their husbands. It shows in the husband's tone of voice, shortness of speech, lack of gentleness and consideration for the wife's feelings and interests. *The root of the problem is that the husband has minimal sensitivity toward God.* He sees his self-sufficient, objective, unemotional way of life as an evidence of strength. In God's sight it is a fatal weakness.

To what degree has God been able to break your heart by giving you an awareness of your proud self-sufficient spirit? One of the tragedies of today is the absence of weeping over our sinfulness. Tears are looked upon as weakness. And in striving to become strong, successful, and personally adequate we turn from the path of child-like trust and implicit dependence on God. Our hearts become hard and our spirits become unfeeling. We forget that "The sacrifices of God are a broken spirit: a broken and contrite heart, O God, thou wilt not despise." Psalms 51:17

You cannot be truly right with God and essentially wrong in your marriage. *What you express in your relationships to your wife will be the overflow of what is true in your heart.* If God has given you a tender, feeling, child-like spirit toward Himself, you will be tender, sensitive and appreciative toward your other self — your wife.

So, if you are hung-up because you can't understand your wife emotionally; if you find that you tune her out, are insensitive to her feelings, and critical of her unpredictable nature; it is quite possible that you are hard toward God and calloused toward a loving Saviour.

206

You and I are a part of our society which inevitably leaves its imprint on our character. This is a materialistic age. We have made a goddess of material success. A part of our culture is the mad drive to acquire material possessions. We become like that which we love. And to love *things* supremely is to become, like them, hard, cold and unfeeling.

What is the answer to your hardness toward your wife's emotional nature? It will not be found in trying to figure out what makes her function as she does, but rather in having the depths of your own emotion stirred by the mighty love of God. Ask Him to give you an awareness of your sinfulness as He sees and feels it. Plead with Him for the ability to weep over the hurts and the lostness of men around you. Jesus wept over the lostness of Jerusalem. Can you weep over the lostness of your neighbors?

Let your emotions be stirred in your relationship to God's concerns and men's condition, and you will find a new tenderness blossoming within you toward your wife.

# 19

# Wow!

### That Other Woman

It developed so imperceptibly, gathering hidden momentum, then showing itself in a variety of seemingly insignificant ways. Suddenly it burst upon his consciousness with the fury of a tornado, and entranced his whole being like the warm disarming breeze of early spring.

Don suddenly found himself overcome. She was in his thoughts by day and in his dreams at night. He found a thousand reasons for thinking of her and longed desperately to be with her. And when circumstances threw them together there was that desperate urge to take her in his arms and possess her to the full.

There was nothing wrong at home. Jody was the same faithful loving wife she'd always been. She gave no evidence of even suspecting the titanic struggle Don was going through. What a shock it would have been had she known Don was in love with another woman!

208

*Wow!*

What are the reasons so many husbands go through such an experience? And what are the answers? What should you do when you find all unexpectedly there's another attraction on your horizon?

It's happening every day — at all married age levels — young couples, middle age, and the elderly. The fact that it hasn't happened to you, and that you've vowed it won't, is no proof it won't happen.

In Don's case there was a happy ending. The spell of emotion was broken, the infatuation passed, and Don emerged a stronger, wiser and more mature person for the experience. But tragically for all too many the ending is not so happy. If the marriage isn't shattered it often suffers deep, almost irreparable damage. Scars are inflicted that may last a life time.

## WHY?

We live in a tragically superficial society. The appeals of billboards and magazine advertisements, of television programs and commercials, of book titles and their contents are geared increasingly to the momentary, the fleeting, the whimsical. The thrust is to treat life lightly and to handle the sober realities of life carelessly.

There are some stubborn facts of life. One of these is that men and women are constituted biologically attractive. Like the two wires leading to the light fixture: touch their bare ends and you'll have sparks. Strangely enough the "spark" doesn't happen every time a man and woman are together. There is a mystery that makes man-woman relationships unpredictable. *But the potential for sexual arousal is latent in every adult.*

209

The ignorance of this fact or the refusal to accept it accounts in part for the surprise and shock that many experience when they suddenly awaken to a growing interest in a person other than their spouse. As one put it,

"How could this happen to me? I had no thoughts of intimacy toward the man. We were good friends and we enjoyed each other's company. Suddenly things got out of hand, and I find myself pregnant."

When will people start taking their biological dynamite seriously?

Many people have a false idealism about men, women and sex. They believe a person who's really right with God won't be attracted to an illegitimate object. To feel attracted, they believe, is a sign of spiritual weakness. Also, they think the *feeling* is itself sinful. This compounds the problem and multiplies the guilt.

Others believe that marriage, when adequate, automatically solves the problem, and so the happily married couple often least suspect their own individual vulnerability.

Never in history has there been such a mobile society with such open permissiveness. The external protective pressures designed to keep people in the straight and narrow path have almost disappeared. Friendships are casual and shallow. There is a free mixing of the sexes, a general lack of deep Christian character and an absence of the fear of God. The emphasis on the importance and desirability of excitement in sexual encounter works to encourage freedom in relationships outside of marriage. Many a man has fallen in trouble simply because he didn't use common sense or pay attention to the subtle warning signals flashing within him.

210

There is also the tragic reality of multiplying marriage inadequacies. While having a wholesome marriage doesn't guarantee you won't be drawn to another woman, having an unhappy marriage really multiplies your chances for such an attraction.

The Bible makes it clear that God intended marriage to provide all that men and women need from each other emotionally and sexually. This is what Paul means in I Corinthians 7:3–5:

"Let the husband render unto the wife her due: and likewise also the wife unto the husband. The wife hath not power over her own body, but the husband: and likewise also the husband hath not power over his own body, but the wife.

"Defraud ye not one the other, except it be by consent for a season, that ye may give yourselves unto prayer, and may be together again, that Satan tempt you not because of your incontinency."

The same truth is stated in Proverbs 5:15–20:

"Drink waters out of thine own cistern. And running waters out of thine own well. Should thy springs be dispersed abroad. And streams of water in the streets? Let them be for thyself alone, and not for strangers with thee. Let thy fountain be blessed; And rejoice in the wife of thy youth. As a loving hind and a pleasant doe, Let her breasts satisfy thee at all times; And be thou ravished always with her love. For why shouldest thou, my son, be ravished with a strange woman, And embrace the bosom of a foreigner?"

It's fatal to be casual or careless about your marriage! Don't take it for granted. Love is a very tender plant; it needs lots of cultivating.

Another reason underlying the problem of "the other woman" is our false idea of what love is. If love is emotion and emotion is love, then as soon as you have emotional stirrings toward a woman not your wife, very naturally you have a problem. If at the same time your affections toward your wife are quiet or seemingly non-existent, you may start assuming you are falling in love. Attention to this only increases the feelings.

Since American marriages are supposedly based on being in love with a person, then almost automatically you may start thinking of ways to terminate the "loveless" relationship and marry the latest woman you have "fallen" in love with.

> Walt was in Christian work, married, and the father of a son in his late teens. His marriage had been stormy, although areas of conflict had been resolved, including earlier sexual difficulties. But to Walt the marriage was increasingly empty, for he felt deep in his heart that he didn't really love his wife.
>
> In time he met and fell in love with a young woman in Christian service. Since he was in love with her, he followed his feelings, tried to divorce his wife and marry the girl. The young lady conceived a child by Walt who, too late, found he couldn't obtain a divorce.

The scars inflicted on all the participants in this unhappy story may never be erased in this life. But a part of the problem was rooted in Walt's mistaken idea of love.

While emotion is a part of true love, it is only a part. You and I are to be *masters of our emotions,* not their slaves. Emotion is to be our servant, not our tyrant.

212

## HOW

1. You must start by accepting the fact that the capacity to be attracted to women is God-given and pure in itself. But God ordained that this drive is to be exercised toward one person only — your wife.

There is a *set of the mind and will* which the Bible describes in very vivid terms:

> "Even so reckon ye also yourselves to be dead unto sin, but alive unto God in Christ Jesus."    Romans 6:11

> "for if ye live after the flesh, ye must die; but if by the Spirit ye put to death the deeds of the body, ye shall live."
> Romans 8:13

> "And they that are of Christ Jesus have crucified the flesh with the passions and the lusts thereof."    Galatians 5:24

> "Put to death therefore your members which are upon the earth: fornication, uncleanness, passion, evil desire, and covetousness, which is idolatry."    Colossians 3:5 ff

These passages applied mean that you must have it settled once for all that *yielding* to an illicit attraction is sin. Even if you don't get physically involved, but merely indulge yourself mentally with someone not your wife, that indulgence is sin.

The *capacity* to be attracted is *not* sin. Nor is the object (another woman who attracts you) evil. The sinfulness lies in your inward yielding to indulge the attraction.

2. Renew your commitment to your wife as your *only* intimate companion. This must be accompanied by implicit faith in God's promise: "Sin shall not have dominion over you, because you are not under law (demands

for performance) but under grace (freely given power to perform)." Romans 6:14

This means you must immediately place the whole situation in God's hands, believing He is giving you, right *now*, the power to refuse the temptation to indulge the attraction.

The temptation itself may not leave. You may find yourself desperately wanting to indulge in mental fantasy and imagine yourself romantically involved with the person. Or you may be tempted to condemn yourself for being so evil minded. You may even plot secretly how you could become intimate with her without making a fool of yourself and ruining everything. But hold persistently to two settled facts:

a. You are committed to do what is right, which automatically precludes any possibility of indulging your desire.

b. Christ has promised to keep you. Hold firm, expecting Him to undertake for you. Thank Him that He *is now keeping you*. Praise Him that the power of sin *has been broken*. Reaffirm the fact that you have died to sin through being joined to Christ. Remember the battle is a *fight of faith,* not a struggle to be good. Unbelief is your real enemy, not your passion or her attractiveness. But don't keep looking at your amount of faith. Look at the power of the One you are trusting.

"Cast not away therefore your boldness, which hath great recompense of reward. For ye have need of steadfastness, that, having done the will of God (trusted Christ in this matter) ye may receive the promise." (victory over the temptation) Hebrews 10:35,36

3. While "fighting the good fight of faith" you need to cultivate your own love garden. "Gird up the loins of your mind" (I Peter 1:6) and redirect your thinking.

   a. Thank God for your wife.
   b. List her positive qualities, and spend time thinking about them and being thankful for them.
   c. Do little things that express love to her.
   d. Spend time courting her and let her satisfy you sexually.

A team of men involved in God's work would be away from home for weeks at a time. But they were alert to the dangers inherent in this kind of ministry. Very wisely they agreed to watch over each other. If at any time a team member noticed one of the men looking too much at young ladies, it would be suggested that maybe the fellow's wife was getting lonely and a break would be arranged.

Weeds grow without cultivation, and wild passion can flourish when love at home is neglected.

4. Be honest about the negatives in your marriage. Identify them and make a list of them. List the things about your wife you consider negatives, but do it only after listing the positives.

Be sure you see her negatives in proportion. Maybe you've made mountains out of mole-hills.

One day Pam came to Jill for counseling. She began by complaining about what a terrible husband she had.

"Oh," said Jill, "Is he an alcoholic?"

"Oh no," replied Pam, "He wouldn't touch the stuff."

"Wonderful," said Jill, "Then your husband is a sober man. You ought to be thankful for that. Does he beat you?"

"No," said Pam, "He wouldn't touch me."

"You're fortunate, your husband doesn't drink and he doesn't beat you. You ought to be thankful."

"Does he let the family go hungry?" my wife continued.

"Well, no, he's a good provider," Pam answered.

"Why Pam, shouldn't you thank God for a man who's a good provider?"

"Does he run with other women?" pursued Jill.

"No . . . I'm sure he's completely faithful."

"Just think Pam, in these few minutes we've found some wonderful positives about your husband. I think you are a very fortunate woman who ought to be thanking God for giving you such a fine man."

It was as though scales dropped from Pam's eyes. She hadn't been cultivating her love-garden. The weeds of idle thoughts had concentrated on romantic ideas so she couldn't see the roses blooming in her husband's character.

Of course the negatives are there in your wife. They exist in you too. And there'll be just as many in the woman to whom you are drawn! But negatives are not solved by brooding over them and hating the person because of them. They can only be resolved by:

First, seeing them in balance and for what they *really* are in the light of the total person and her positives.

Second, lovingly, patiently and prayerfully dealing with them and/or your attitude toward them.

Always remember, God loves your wife *with her negatives,* and He's asking her to love you *with your negatives.* Can His love in your heart love her too? Try to see her through the eyes and heart of Jesus. Like the woman Jill

216

talked to, you might be surprised what a treasure you have within your own wife!

5. Be honest and realistic about actual inadequacies in your marriage. These can unconsciously provide a seed bed for temptation.

Bill was a good provider, faithful in every way, but as a person he was matter-of-fact and somewhat non-verbal. As an advancing engineer with increasing responsibilities in his job he didn't realize how much he took his attractive, talented wife for granted.

Chris, his wife, was not only attractive and talented, but she also had a deep need for attention and appreciation.

Bill's absorption in his work, and his matter-of-fact approach to life nearly cost him what he had felt was a very satisfying marriage.

Little did he dream his wife had the right ingredients to elicit a "wow!" from another man. One day it happened. Chris felt lonely, unappreciated, unneeded. They passed in the hall — Chris and the "other" man. He too was lonely, taken for granted, and unappreciated. Suddenly he "saw" Chris. A bright smile, a cheery voice with those appreciative words: "You're looking mighty sharp!" and the match was lit. Two married people, both earnest Christians, were caught in the violent vortex of mind numbing attraction for each other. It went almost too far, and only by a miracle were they saved from marital disaster.

In one sense Bill had himself to blame. Yes, the "other man" was wrong — totally so. And so was Chris. But had Bill been alert to an area of inadequacy in his marriage, Chris may never have responded to the "other man's" cheerful note of commendation and attention.

217

*Specifics*

So check out the weak areas. Discuss them with your wife. You need to be open with each other and face with maturity any area where inadequacy in your marriage may leave a loop-hole for temptation for either one of you.

If you aren't satisfied emotionally or sexually you have an obligation to be honest and open with your wife about it. Don't build up resentment toward her in a brooding silence. She may be oblivious to your desires, or there may be attitudes and actions on your part that make it difficult for her to be warm and loving. Perhaps she has mental or psychological hang-ups about sex which she has never discussed with you.

Settle once and for all that God gave you to one another for the express purpose of each completing the other as married partners. So face whatever areas of inadequacy you may have, and recognize *you each have the God-given potential for being an adequate partner.* Accept the fact too that *you don't need anything more in marriage than your wife is able to give.*

This last statement may shock you. There are thousands of men *and* women who feel they've been short-changed in marriage. Maybe you're one of those husbands who feels he's been cheated. But I *didn't* say every wife is to her husband all he *wants!* I said he doesn't *need in marriage* more than she is *able* to give.

We need to keep two things clear. There is a difference between *needs* and *wants.* You and I have to *evaluate our wants* in terms of the objectives and values of the kingdom of God to which we belong.

In our materialistic society we have almost forgotten

that old fashioned, "holy contentment," of which Paul spoke in I Timothy 6:6–9:

> "But godliness with contentment is great gain: for we brought nothing into the world, for neither can we carry anything out; but having food and covering we shall be therewith content. But they that are minded to be rich fall into a temptation and a snare and many foolish and hurtful lusts, such as drown men in destruction and perdition."

The principle expressed in this passage applies to much more than hankering after money or the things money can buy. It applies to every area of life.

The adequate marriage is being presented today as an exciting, non-monotonous, continually "turned on" sort of relationship.* So, if your wife doesn't excite you (whether physically, mentally, emotionally or sexually), you are supposed to assume your marriage is inadequate. This idea alone can cause you to "look again" at another woman who seems to have the "it" your wife is missing.

Take all your "wants" in marriage to the Lord. Talk to Him about them. He might show you you don't need all you *want*. In fact, one of the purposes of redemption is to deliver us from being slaves to our wants. And if you'll be honest with God, and willing for His will, He'll show you the balance between legitimate needs and over-developed, demanding, but unnecessary wants.

* Note: The same idea is being presented as the ideal relationship to Christ. i.e. — if your Christian life isn't *exciting*, there's something wrong with it. We are to walk faithfully with God because it is *right* to do so; not because it is exciting. There is much in Christian living that is routine, drab, and unexciting.

*Specifics*

After you've honestly talked to God about your being short-changed, then discuss with your wife those areas where you feel you need more from her in marriage.

If you will be honest with each other and with God, *and are willing to work together* in an attitude of love and trust in the Lord, there are very few genuine needs that married partners *cannot* fulfill for each other.

6. Be sensible. It's amazing how we create trouble for ourselves by our foolish and unwise ways. It is seldom that a man has to continue in positions that stimulate awakened interest in a woman. If you *have* to drive her home, get your wife to go with you, or call a taxi for her. There are thousands of ways you can get on thin ice, but for every one there is also a way to stay off it. Ask God to give you common sense! Always remember *you are vulnerable.*

7. Take a wholesome, positive attitude toward the person who's attracting you. Thank God she's attractive, then remind God and yourself that she's *not* for you.

8. As long as the battle is in your own heart and mind, don't tell the woman about it, nor your wife. To do so is to hurt both of them unnecessarily. Scars will be inflicted needlessly, and you will put them both into unpredictable conflicts. Satan may get an advantage in ways you may not have dreamed.

If you've yielded to your feelings, and overt indiscreet actions have been done, you may need to make amends. But insofar as possible, avoid any further involvement.

Too often a man thinks primarily about himself, his own guilt and its alleviation. But true love seeks what is best for the one loved, and you need to ask yourself and

220

God, will your comtemplated action result in good for your wife and/or the woman you have been drawn to?

9. Don't beat yourself if you have been attracted and have indulged the attraction secretly. Be honest with yourself and with God about it. Claim His forgiveness and cleansing, and get on with "fighting the good fight of faith", i.e. *expecting* His deliverance. Keep praising God that He *is* keeping you *now*. If need be get alone somewhere and shout your praise audibly. Tell God you believe Him. Take a leaf out of Abraham's experience in Romans 4:19–21:

> "And without being weakened in faith he considered his own body now as good as dead (he being about a hundred years old), and the deadness of Sarah's womb; yet, looking unto the promise of God, he wavered not through unbelief, but waxed strong through faith, giving glory to God, and being fully assured that what He had promised, He was able also to perform."

From all external appearances there was no hope that he could become a father through Sarah his wife. But by steadfastly looking at God's promise, and by assuring himself of God's integrity through affirming it verbally, his faith grew and in due course the promise was fulfilled.

Faith is an active, aggressive, militant dynamic. It is not passive. Let this experience make you a stronger man and a more mature Christian.

10. Be sure you don't indulge a critical, condemning attitude toward others who have yielded to an illicit attraction. Paul warns about this:

"Wherefore let him that thinketh he standeth take heed lest he fall."                                                  I Corinthians 10:12

"Brethren, even if a man be overtaken in any trespass, ye who are spiritual restore such a one in a spirit of gentleness; looking to thyself, lest thou also be tempted."

Galatians 6:1

If by experience you have found that your safety is in God's keeping power and not in your own dogged determination, you should be a much more understanding, patient, and helpful brother to another who is going through one of life's toughest battle areas.

# Part V

Thoughts on the Why of It All

# 20

# That Your Prayers Be Not Hindered

Most men need reasons for things. It's important to know the why. If the reason appears valid and sufficiently important, a thinking man will usually take notice.

There are many books available that talk about the family, and they say many good and important things. But *WHY* must the home be all we are saying it should be? *Why must it be Godly?* Ask yourself that question. Better yet, make it the subject of an after-dinner family discussion!

You'd probably come up with a variety of answers — most of which, I suspect, could be summarized under the general heading, "So we can all be happy". That's great as far as it goes. But does it go far enough?

Remember back in chapter three, we talked about the system being twisted? At the heart of life is a cancer.

*The Why of it All*

Its name is selfishness. You want what you want and I want what I want. The difficulty is we each want different things! What is happiness to one person may be misery to another.

Jill and I were flying over the rugged Canadian Rockies. It was early winter and snow was already heavy at the higher elevations.

"Fantastic!" I exclaimed.

"Cruel," Jill replied.

"Majestic," I countered.

"Cold and forbidding," she retorted.

"I love them," said I.

"I recoil from them," she shuddered.

"Wouldn't it be great to live in them?" I suggested.

"Miserable," she answered.

In the degree to which our individual ideas of happiness differ we may find happiness proportionately difficult to discover.

Consequently wanting happiness is not an adequate reason for giving attention to your home and in particular to your role as husband and father.

An adequate reason for being, relating, and acting in a given way in the family must have several elements:

1. It must be worthy of the God-created nature of each individual in the family.
2. It must be in harmony with a clear conscience.
3. It must benefit all members of the family, not just one or two.
4. It must be rooted in what God in the Bible says about the family.

We are commanded in I Peter 3:7:

"Ye husbands, in like manner, dwell with your wives according to *knowledge*, giving honor unto the woman, as unto the weaker vessel, as being also joint-heirs of the grace of life; to the end that your prayers be not hindered."

Here is one basic reason why you and I as husbands are to have wholesome relationships with our wives — so our prayers will be effective. Wow! Had you ever seen that? When I did, it put family relationships in a totally different light. In effect it said:

"Fred, you are to live with Jill with the kind of understanding and consideration that creates an atmosphere in your home which is conducive to God hearing and answering your prayers."

This lifts family living way above the realm of human selfishness. In fact it takes us clear back to the garden of Eden, where God assigned to that first family the tremendous responsibility of ruling this world for Him (Genesis 1:28). In other words we are to live in our families in a way that makes it possible to fulfill the purposes for which God created mankind in the first place!

There is something more important than being happy. It is to fulfill our reason for being. Happiness is a fruit, not a root; an effect, not a cause.

One reason there is so much *unhappiness* in marriage is because we have made happiness the goal. And for all too many that goal has been like the elusive pot of gold at the end of the rainbow.

True happiness is the result of fulfilling prior conditions, of pursuing higher goals. The principle was expressed by Jesus in several vivid statements:

*The Why of it All*

"For whosoever would save his life shall lose it; but whosoever shall lose his life for my sake, the same shall save it."

Luke 9:24

". . . Except a grain of wheat fall into the earth and die, it abideth by itself alone; but if it die, it beareth much fruit."

John 12:24

"And whosoever shall exalt himself shall be humbled; and whosoever shall humble himself shall be exalted."

Matthew 23:12

Each of these statements refers to men pursuing the wrong goals, and as a result losing them.

But why put such importance on having our prayers answered? There are at least two reasons:

1. It *shows* man is in touch with God. The ultimate evidence that a person is rightly related to God is the fact that God responds when such a person talks to Him. To pray is one thing. And millions pray. But to have our prayers acknowledged by response from the infinite God is quite something else. Comparatively few know much about this response.

2. To fulfill man's purpose for being, which is to function as God's representative in a physical world. Since we are only finite beings, beset with the frailties of human nature, there is no way we could possibly fulfill God's command, "Rule this world for me," unless God should stand behind our actions. But here is where the New Testament Christians found their strength — in keeping with promises given by Jesus:

"I will give unto thee the keys of the kingdom of heaven: and whatsoever thou shalt bind on earth shall be bound in

228

heaven; and whatsoever thou shalt loose on earth shall be loosed in heaven." Matthew 16:19

"Verily I say unto you, What things soever ye shall bind on earth shall be bound in heaven; and what things soever ye shall loose on earth shall be loosed in heaven. Again I say unto you, that if two of you shall agree on earth as touching anything that they shall ask, it shall be done for them of my Father who is in heaven. For where two or three are gathered together in my name, there am I in the midst of them." Matthew 18:18–20

"Whose soever sins ye forgive, they are forgiven unto them; whose soever sins ye retain, they are retained." John 20:23

"Rejoice over her, thou heaven, and ye saints, and ye apostles, and ye prophets; for God hath judged your judgment on her." Revelation 18:20

The early Christians experienced the realities expressed in these statements. God worked in response to their will. For them prayer was more than asking. In prayer they affirmed that God's will should be done. Because they were in tune with God and His will, their faith enabled them to decree with boldness that what God had willed should come to pass.

The early church was a hunted, hounded despised minority. It had nothing going for it except the reality of the power and love of God. Their resources were "other worldly." And with those resources nothing could stop the triumphant march of the church's glorious influence. Within the first century the effects of Christ's redeeming, transforming power had been felt at all levels of society and to the farthest reaches of the then known world!

The secret of it all was in the growing number of

229

"house churches," at times only the family. In them there was such a spirit of love, understanding, and harmony that nothing hindered the free flow of relationship between the Lord of heaven and His people. As each Christian home decreed in believing prayer that the will of God be done, God would work in response to what His people prayed.

That prayer *was* a significant factor in those early Christian homes is implied in Paul's directions to husbands and wives in I Corinthians 7:3–5:

> "Let the husband render unto the wife her due; and likewise also the wife unto the husband. The wife hath not power over her own body, but the husband: and likewise also the husband hath not power over his own body, but the wife. Defraud ye not one the other, except it be by consent for a season, *that ye may give yourselves unto prayer,* and may be together again, that Satan tempt you not because of your incontinency."

Paul here tells Christian couples not to interrupt regular sexual intercourse except for one mutually agreed upon reason: to be free to have prolonged, uninterrupted prayer times! He doesn't indicate whether such praying was to be together, separately, just one being involved or both. But regardless of the pattern, the fact that he mentions prolonged prayer as the only legitimate interrupter of family intimacies is evidence that such praying must have been common for those Christian households.

What a reason for living harmoniously! To make it possible for you and me in our families and in our hectic day to fulfill our God-given reason for being. And how?

by living as His representative in a fallen world, and through prayer insisting that:

— His Name be held in reverence in this world.
— His lordship be established in men's hearts.
— His will be done in this world just as it's done so gladly and fully in heaven.                                    Matthew 6:9–10

This reason for having a right kind of family relationship is both valid and adequate.

1. It is worthy of our nature as being created in God's image, and who through faith in Jesus Christ are now sons of the living God.
2. It satisfies conscience.
3. It results in good for our families and all mankind.
4. It is rooted in what God has revealed in the Bible.

The highest kind of happiness is bound to flow in that home where this reason for wholesome relationships motivates its members.

Where relationships with your wife and children are not right, effective prayer is impossible. But if your heart is right toward God the Holy Spirit will be faithful to make clear to you specifically what the hinderance is. Not once but many times I have had to stop attempting to pray until some matter between my wife and me was made right. I recall one incident when it seemed like God was speaking directly to me:

"Stop praying and go ask your wife's forgiveness!"

"But I was right and she was wrong," I replied.

"But your spirit was wrong," God seemed to say.

"If I apologize to her, she will run the place," I argued.

231

"Never mind who runs the place," God responded. "Go and do what I tell you."

We cannot fulfill our purpose in life as God's representatives in this world unless we are in harmony with Him, and are willing to respond by obedience to His directives when He speaks. And one of these directives commands you and me to dwell with our wives according to knowledge, giving them honor and acknowledging their equality with us in the kingdom of God. (I Peter 3:7)

How well do you know and understand your wife? Do you see her as a person just as important to God as you are?

Specifically, how much have you consciously tried to understand her?

Do you discuss with her the areas where she is a mystery to you?

But more than just understanding her, you are to live with your wife on the basis of that understanding. That is, you are to adjust your behavior to harmonize with her nature.

There *are* differences between men and women. I am to give my wife the *right* to be different and relate to her positively in the areas of those differences.

On a visit to South Africa Jill and I were being shown through a wild animal park. We enjoyed to the full being able to see the various animals living in their native habitat. But when we came to the reptile house, Jill drew back. She has an instinctive horror of snakes. To me they are fascinating, even though I want to stay at a distance from them.

To live with my wife according to knowledge involved giving her the full right to decline going into that reptile

232

house — and to do so without her fearing ridicule or some other negative reaction from me.

The Holy Spirit is grieved and effective prayer is hindered more often by *little ways* in which you and I as husbands fail to give our wives honor in the areas of their differences, which often appear to us as weakness. Remember, she is equally with you an heir of the grace of life. Where two of you, God's children, are at odds, even in seemingly small matters, He cannot respond freely to your prayers.

The *purposes* of God are fulfilled through *both husband and wife as a unit, not through one or the other as individuals.* This is the root reason why your home *must* be godly.

# 21

# You Both Need Climate to Grow In

In the beginning God said it wasn't good for man to
be alone. (Genesis 2:15) He wasn't referring only to man's
need for human companionship. He was saying Adam
wasn't complete in himself. He needed another person to
complete him. This is the real meaning of the statement:

"I will make for Adam a help suited to his needs."
Genesis 1:18

Since Adam wasn't complete in himself, neither was
Eve. That first family, perfect and pure from God's cre-
ative hand was mutually inter-dependent. Adam and
Eve needed each other!

Individual personal fulfillment would be dependent
on the degree to which they would grow into the oneness
which was to have begun at marriage.

234

"Therefore shall a man leave his father and mother, and shall cleave unto his wife: and they shall be one flesh."

Genesis 2:24

This is another important reason why relationships in our homes *must* be right; to create an atmosphere conducive to wholesome personality development of both husband and wife.

People, like plants, need climate in which to develop.

My hobby is flowers. For many years, we had a small greenhouse attached to our family room. My constant concern was to provide in that greenhouse the kind of climate most suitable to the nature of the plants I was growing. Given favorable conditions, I had the delight of watching the flowers unfold in all their exquisite beauty. Sometimes I missed it. Instead of beauty, the flowers were deformed, incomplete, and at times the buds shriveled.

The potential for beauty was in the plant, but without the proper climate the potential failed to be realized.

Every person has a God-given potential for beauty in his or her personality. As separate individuals alone, living by ourselves, there is a degree to which this potential can be realized. But the *full blossoming* of man's personality into all God designed it to be is possible only within the mysterious oneness of husband and wife in marriage. While there are exceptions, they are not the rule. You are a part of your wife and your wife is a part of you. Given the right conditions, what you give to each other will result in the unfolding of both of your personalities with a beauty that fulfills the potential God planted within you at birth.

Paul talks about this in his letter to the Christians at Epheus, Chapter 5: verses 21–33 K.J.V.

"Submitting yourselves one to another in the fear of God. Wives, submit yourselves unto your own husbands, as unto the Lord. For the husband is the head of the wife, even as Christ is the head of the church; and he is the saviour of the body. Therefore as the church is subject unto Christ, so let the wives be to their own husbands in everything. Husbands, love your wives, even as Christ also loved the church, and gave Himself for it; that He might sanctify and cleanse it with the washing of water by the word, that He might present it to Himself a *glorious church,* not having spot, or wrinkle, or any such thing; but that it should be holy and *without blemish.* So ought men to love their wives as their own bodies. He that loveth his wife loveth himself. For no man ever yet hated his own flesh; but nourisheth and cherisheth it, even as the Lord the church: For we are members of His body, of His flesh, and of His bones. For this cause shall a man leave his father and mother, and shall be joined unto his wife, and they two shall be one flesh. This is a great mystery, but I speak concerning Christ and the church. Nevertheless, let every one of you in particular so love his wife even as himself; and the wife see that she reverence her husband."

In this passage, Paul says there are two elements that are basic to wholesome husband-wife relationships: joyful abandonment by the wife to her husband, and purposeful, self-giving love of the husband to his wife. Each is to give himself wholly and equally to the other, but in two different dimensions.

## JOYFUL ABANDONMENT

For the wife God commands a willing, joyful abandonment — a losing of herself in her husband. This is expressed by the command:

"Wives submit yourselves unto your own husbands *as unto the Lord.*"  Ephesians 5:22

God will not accept from us a reluctant, half-hearted, forced surrender to Himself. The only submission He accepts is a glad, free, wholehearted love-abandonment. This is to be so total that it is described as the Christian being one spirit with the Lord.

"He that is joined to the Lord is one spirit."  I Corinthians 6:17

So wives are to become *one in spirit with their husbands,* by a voluntary, glad, wholehearted abandonment to them. Involved in this relationship is a loyalty, a reality of being so one with her husband, that he is set free to be himself. He is delivered from all fear of his wife as a competitor, a rival, or a person whose identification with himself must be bargained for, earned, or preserved only by dint of great effort.

Many, if not most men are afraid of their wives. Women are usually strong in personality, if not in body. They function differently than men, and often appear inscrutably mysterious to their husbands. Women are just as gifted as men, and in some areas more so.

In far more ways than most husbands care to admit, their wives are a threat to them. For many this threat is totally unrecognized by the husband and certainly is not

237

deliberate for most wives. But whether recognized or not, it is there — even though latent.

There is only one way this threat can be removed: Through a work of grace in the wife's heart producing such inward heart abandonment to her husband that she becomes in heart and spirit one with him.

There are two wonderful results from the reality of that abandonment:

1. The husband is set free inwardly to become all God planned he should be when he was created and redeemed by God.
2. The gifts God gave his wife can now be developed and used freely because they have ceased to constitute a threat to her husband. This is because they are used *as a part* of her husband, and no longer as "her thing" to be separate from or competitive to him.

Where identification of a wife with her husband is genuinely the result of God's work in her life, the question of order, authority and roles becomes essentially academic.

## SELF-GIVING LOVE

For the husband God commands a self-giving, purposeful, redemptive love toward his wife.

"Husbands, love your wives even as Christ also loved the church, and gave Himself up for it."      Ephesians 5:25

In the very nature of marriage the abandonment we have discussed is frightening to a wife. Historically men have dominated women in varying degrees. The nature of this domination ranges from tyrannical subjugation, to condescending toleration. The former enslaves her, physically and mentally as demonstrated in many non-Christian societies. The latter treats her as useful for limited functions, but certainly not equal to man in ability or status. This attitude has been more common in western culture including that which has called itself Christian.

Women must be strong to defend themselves against sexual abuse, since they are the sufferers when sexually assaulted and impregnated. What can a man really know of the burden, pain and fears of child-bearing? Created sexually aggressive, it is comparatively easy for a man to force himself on his wife, then to let her suffer the consequences of his act while he gets on with whatever he wishes.

The problem of wholesome relationships is complicated by our native self-centeredness. Even a man's love for his wife is distorted by selfishness, so that his innate ideas above love focus on what he is to *get* from loving rather than what he can *give* to his wife as her lover.

The answer to the seemingly hopeless barrier to husband-wife oneness has been demonstrated by Christ Himself. The key is found, for husbands, in the command:

"Husbands love your wives *as Christ also loved the church.*"
Ephesians 5:25

The Bible states and experience demonstrates that selfgiving, purposeful love is the only dynamic that allays suspicion, quiets fear, disarms resistance, and induces a response of glad abandonment and total loyalty.

"We love, because He first loved us."  I John 4:19

"Not that we loved God, but that He loved us and sent His son to be the propitiation for our sin."  I John 4:10

"There is no fear in love: but perfect love casts out fear. . ."  I John 4:18

Love creates a climate of safety and freedom. Within the climate of Christ's love, rebellious, self-loving, God-suspicious man find's himself capitulating to the eternal God who is seen no longer as an awesome tyrant, but as the Eternal Lamb! This love is not a velvet glove covering a mailed fist of steel, or the hardness of a cushioned brick. It has a different nature. Christ's love does not *hide* a terror side of God. It shows the *real* nature of God which is *not terror but omnipotent strength which blesses*. God is terror *only to those who hate good and who thereby delight in hurting*. (John 3:19–20) His terror therefore is an expression of His love. And to all who choose good (that which is genuinely right), God's total being is seen as loving and infinitely blessed.

It is with this kind of love that we husbands are to love our wives. In this love there is no selfishness, but rather self-giving. It's objective is the wife's well being. This love sets a man's wife free — free to become all God had in mind she should become when He created her, redeemed her, and joined her to her husband. She is free to grow, to blossom, to unfold as the flower to the sunshine.

And in that unfolding she becomes the completer of her husband.

In the degree to which there is this positive relationship between a man and his wife, a climate is created for mutual growth and fulfillment.

In this climate there is freedom to be ourselves. This includes the freedom to fail, to be weak, to make mistakes. There is freedom to be different, and to have different gifts. Each will be the better for having married the other. And through a couple's deepening oneness, blessing flows out to others in an ever widening circle.

This reason for having a right relationship with your wife also meets the criteria stated in chapter twenty.

    a. It is worthy of the God-created nature of both the husband and his wife.
    b. Conscience approves it wholeheartedly.
    c. It results in good to all who are involved in it.
    d. It is thoroughly Biblical. As Christ and the church are one and interdependent, so a man and his wife are to be one and interdependent.

Are you and your wife better people for having married each other?

In order for a person to grow he must be free to need to grow. Does your wife have that freedom?

Is it totally safe for your wife to abandon herself to you? Not only in sex, but in every other area of her life?

What does your love do to her? For her?

Are you free and secure in the climate of your wife's acceptance and loyalty? Are you a better person because of her?

Do you secretly fear her abilities? Or do you encourage her to develop them and use them?

Can you fail safely?

Could you and your wife discuss freely and wholesomely the contents of chapters twenty and twenty one?

Will you?

When?

What a change came into our own home when God enabled
us to get the two basic elements of climate sorted out. For
me it meant letting go of my own self-centeredness which
made my love turn sour whenever it wasn't responded to in
a way that pleased me. It involved a heart-identification with
Jill as she was, not as I wanted her to be. I had to accept her
as a part of myself, so that her weaknesses became mine,
her failures mine, and her sins became my sins as well. I
began to use "we" language instead of "her" and "me" language.

For Jill it meant accepting me as I was, abandoning herself
to me in my non-ideal condition and trusting God to work
out life situations where I had fouled them up, instead of
pushing, nagging, or criticizing me for what I had done
wrong.

A new climate of trust and oneness made mutual growth
and maturing an ongoing reality instead of an idyllic dream.
And on the foundation of that deepening oneness our di-
vergent gifts and formerly clashing personalities began to
be used by God to bless others. We don't need to haggle
over roles or worry about who should make what decisions.
Life for us flows in a variety of expressions and directions,
but it flows from a single spring created by Christ's love and
power through his fusing of two incomplete people into an
increasingly harmonious whole.

"They two shall become one flesh. . ." and where the body
is a coordinated unit, there is no occasion for jealousy, fear,
resentment, or bickering on the part of each other, yet we
are free to be ourselves for each other. *Only in this way* is it
possible for us to complete each other and thus as a unit fulfill God's will for us in this world.

# 22

# So God Can "Get Through" to Your Children

The negatives of today's society are painfully real to all who have eyes to see. It's into this society our children are born and parents are running scared. But God knew children would be born into a fallen, distorted world. And He lets it happen. Why?

The answer is rooted in a third basic reason why our homes must be godly. Paul expresses it this way in Ephesians 6:4:

> "And you, fathers (parents) don't make your children angry or discouraged, but rear them in the environment of God's correction and instruction." (Paraphrase)

Our homes are to be what they should be so that an atmosphere prevails that is conducive to God having personal dealings with our children.

What a difference between parents dealing with their child and God doing it!

Do you mean parents aren't to instruct, train, correct and discipline their children?

Of course not. The Bible makes it perfectly clear that God holds parents responsible for all that's involved in rearing, training and disciplining their children. This is taught in scripture both by direct command and by illustration.*

The difficulty is we tend to go to one of two extremes. We either ignore our responsibilities for training our children so that they grow up like weeds, or we put all the emphasis on *our* responsibility and forget that our part is to provide a climate in which God Himself can do the vital part of training.

The all important and absolutely essential goal is that the child become a man or woman of God. All other goals must be secondary to this supreme goal.

The only truly stabilizing, preserving dynamic that is adequate for the Christian in a fallen world is a personal knowledge of God Himself. And this knowledge, not *about* God but *of* God, can be communicated to the individual person only by God the Holy Spirit. Even to know the Bible is not in itself to know God!

Here is where many earnest Christians miss the way. They train their children in good habits of behaviour, furnish their minds with an understanding of Bible truths, instill in their wills the habit of making Christian choices, but in the end they miss the heart of it all — the

---

* Genesis 19:19; Deuteronomy 2:18–21; 6:6,7; I Samuel 3:12–14; Proverbs 22:6; 22:15; 23:13,14

imperative of the developing child having personal dealings with God Himself.

The command is to nurture our children in God's dealings with them. This means you and I as fathers have the responsibility of seeing to it that God actually works personally with their developing lives.

But how can we be sure God will do this?

1. By active, aggressive, persistent and believing prayer. Keep reminding God, humbly but boldly, that your children belong to Him and that you agree with God that they should grow up to glorify His name. You must labor in prayer and faith until God responds. "Be not sluggish but imitate them who through faith and steadfastness inherit the promises." Hebrews 6:12

2. You also need to live so that the presence of God is real in your home. Don't settle for correct Christian actions only. Believe God for the awareness at your house that God lives there too. The children will sense this.

3. Don't be content with a "decision for Christ," or even a commitment to Christian service. Keep before God the necessity for true spiritual hunger to develop in your children.

4. Trust the Holy Spirit to show you ways in which you can cooperate with God by naturally and spontaneously bringing God into your conversation and activities.

5. Instead of just correcting a child, you can have them spend some time talking to God about it and together expect God to show them practical steps for improvement. When He answers, take time with them to thank Him.

Upon graduation from high school at eighteen, I announced to my father that I wanted to go to Bible School.

245

"Well, not yet Fred. Your older brothers helped on the farm until you got through school; now it's your turn to help until some of your younger brothers finish. When you're twenty-one you can leave home and go to Bible School."

That was tough for me. I'd milked cows since I was six, and I'd had it with the critters. Anyway I wanted to go to Bible School. But I'd been programmed to obey my dad. In fact it had never seriously occurred to me to disobey him. So I stayed home — but inwardly I was very unhappy.

One day out in the feed lot a voice seemed to say to me:

"Children obey your parents in the Lord for this is right. . ."

"I'm eighteen and no child," I replied.

"Children obey your parents," the voice insisted.

"I'm eighteen and I want to go to Bible School."

"Children obey your parents," came the word again.

Finally I got the message. God was talking. It seemed that my father and his demand became incidental. I was being confronted by someone much greater, and I knew it. At last I yielded and replied to God:

"If I have to stay here until I rot, I won't leave without my father's blessing."

Peace came immediately, and with it a totally new attitude toward the farm, my dad, and life in general. God had spoken. And my staying on that farm was no longer merely obedience to my father's command; it was obedience to the living God.

*     *     *     *     *

As a younger teen I came up against dad's rule that we were not to smoke. Dad didn't mind the innocent fun we had making smokes out of dried corn silk and carrot tops, as long as we didn't set the barn on fire. But he drew the line when it came to the real stuff. As boys we used to gang up on our ponies behind the barn or out in the pasture and some of the neighbor fellows introduced us to real cigarettes. I thought they were great and did I ever feel smart and grown up. Inwardly I was troubled, but I liked the taste of real smoking. One day I found a whole pack — unopened. What a find! I was elated — and troubled. An inward war developed. God seemed to be saying:

"Don't."

"But I want them."

"Get rid of them."

"But I want them."

"You're not to touch them."

"But I want them."

For three days the battle raged as I carried that pack hidden in my pocket. But one morning I knew the issue was settled. Again, it wasn't an issue between dad's rule and me. It was something between me and my awareness of God. He won. On the way to school I pulled that pack from my pocket and threw it as far as I could.

From that day to this tobacco has never been a temptation or an issue.

The foundation of the knowledge of God needs to be established in the lives of our children during their formative years. Of course God can do it later, and many times He does. But this was not His plan. How much better when "The fear of the Lord which is the beginning of wisdom" becomes a growing reality at the outset of behavior pattern development.

Dad, do your children know God lives in your home?

Do they know you fear Him, love Him, trust and obey Him?

Stop a minute. When did you last demonstrate to your children that you really are a reverent, trusting, loving child of God? How did you demonstrate it?

You may teach your children, and they may as easily forget or reject your teaching. A clever professor at college may make them quite confused by his high sounding arguments.

Your moral standards may appear to your young adults as irrelevant and old fashioned.

The exciting drives of youthful appetite may be inflamed into tornadic forces in the free permissive society of that world outside your home.

But there is one lasting, enduring reality your children won't likely forget: The memory of God's reality to you and His personal dealings with them.

The stability of a man's character ultimately is in direct proportion to the reality of his God-granted awareness of God as He truly is.

Is the climate in your home such that beyond all the faithful teaching and training you give your children, God as a person is *getting through* to them?

Your home must be godly so that the foundations of a vital child-God relationship can be built in your children by the Holy Sprit Himself. It is in the home that qualities of godly character, a personal knowledge of Him and reverence for God are to be developed. Then in future years your children as men and women who know their God, can then take their places in an ungodly world and stand true to Him in the deepening darkness.

This final foundation reason for having a godly home, like the other two, is worthy of God who designed the home. Your conscience agrees that the reason is valid. It brings the highest kind of blessing to all in the family, and it certainly accords with the teaching of Scripture.

Where these three conditions prevail in any home, there cannot fail to be the highest kind of happiness:

— A climate that is conducive to God hearing and answering prayer —

— A climate that permits both husband and wife to develop into the people God intended them to be —

— A climate that enables God to have direct personal dealings with the children.

These conditions are at heart the great objective toward which all redemption is moving: the re-establishment of God as a living, abiding, and all pervading Presence in the lives and relationships of His people. Ezekiel states it so beautifully in describing the heavenly Jerusalem:

". . . and the name of the city from that day shall be, Jehovah is there."                    Ezekiel 48:35

Your home must be godly . . . so that all who live in it and those who enter its doors will be aware intuitively that **God is there.**